A FRAMEWORK FOR VISUALIZING INFORMATION

THE KLUWER INTERNATIONAL SERIES ON HCI

VOLUME 1

A Framework for Visualizing Information

by

Ed H. Chi

Xerox Palo Alto Research Center,
Palo Alto, California, U.S.A.

SPRINGER-SCIENCE+BUSINESS MEDIA, B.V.

A C.I.P. Catalogue record for this book is available from the Library of Congress

ISBN 978-90-481-6009-9 ISBN 978-94-017-0573-8 (eBook)
DOI 10.1007/978-94-017-0573-8

Printed on acid-free paper

Originally published by Kluwer Academic Publishers in 2002
Softcover reprint of the hardcover 1st edition 2002

To every blade of grass I've brushed,
To every tree I've touched,
To every water way I've crossed,
To every mountain I've climbed,
To every photograph and step I've taken on this journey

on this amazing planet.

Contents

List of Figures

List of Tables

Declaration

This book is a monograph that was produced by reorganizing and modifying my Ph.D. thesis from March 1999.

The ideas described in this book is patent–pending in a U.S. patent application entitled "Visualization Spreadsheet" (University of Minnesota Docket Number 99009, Merchant & Gould Law Firm Reference Number 600.373-US-01).

Some portion of this book was previous published in IEEE conference proceedings and magazines. As per IEEE Copyright Policy (http://www.computer.org/forminfo.htm), I retained the right to reuse any portion of these copyrighted works, without fee, and in any future works. However, I am required to give the following notice: Some portion of this work is

Preface

Fundamental solutions in understanding information have been elusive for a long time. The field of Artificial Intelligence has proposed the Turing Test as a way to test for the "smart" behaviors of computer programs that exhibit human-like qualities. Equivalent to the Turing Test for the field of Human-Information Interaction (HII), getting information to the people that need them and helping them to understand the information is the new challenge of the Web era.

In a short amount of time, the infrastructure of the Web became ubiquitious not just in terms of protocols and transcontinental cables but also in terms of everyday devices capable of recalling network-stored data, sometimes wirelessly. Therefore, as these infrastructures become reality, our attention on HII issues needs to shift from information *access* to information *sensemaking*, a relatively new term coined to describe the process of digesting information and understanding its structure and intricacies so as to make decisions and take action.

This new focus shift toward sensemaking must involve the improvement of two fundamental issues in HII: input and output. On the *input* side, the problem of devising novel ways of communicating intent and commands to the computer has a long and interesting history. Recent advances in speech, handwriting recognition, and gestures is making great strides toward changing the way we interact with computers. On the *output* side, the fundamental solutions seem to be coming more slowly. Displays remain the primary ways computers communicate information to the user. The evidences so far suggest that this is mainly because the visual channel of human perception has an incredible bandwidth to the cognitive processing centers of the brain. Moreover, it has been used relatively successfully even when the environment is noisy, and when the environment is overloaded with other distractions.

For this very direct reason, the study of visualization or the ability to use vision to think with the aid of computer graphics is important to the advancement of Human-Information Interaction. This monograph is the result of several years of work in which I undertook this challenge with the aid of my colleagues at two institutions—University of Minnesota and Xerox Palo Alto Research Center. The purpose of this monograph is to unify these years of efforts into a single source that can be referenced for future work. In particular, this book describes a visualization reference model that has been invaluable in my own research in thinking about visualization problems. This book further describes a visualization metaphor called "Visualization Spreadsheet", in which I applied this visualization reference model to show how visualization problems can be solved more easily in software systems.

Much work remains to be done. Information Visualization work in the past decade has focused mainly on the desktop environment, where large display surfaces, keyboard, and mice are a given. In addition to the new research needed in mobile device environments, the now prevalent practice of using multiple displays is also fundamentally changing visualization and the way we gather and digest information. It is my hope that the work described in this book will be valuable for new generations of data analysts.

ED H. CHI

Acknowledgments

I specially thank my Ph.D. advisor, John T. Riedl, for his mentorship, support, advice, guidance, encouragement, and above all, his friendship. Choosing him as my advisor was one of the best choices I have made in my life.

In the last several years, I have also been fortunate to have received great mentorship from Stuart Card and Peter Pirolli at Xerox Palo Alto Research Center (Xerox PARC), and I thank them for their belief in my abilities. Jim Pitkow also greatly influenced my work, particularly the research in Web visualization.

I thank Professors John Carlis, Joseph Konstan, and Phillip Barry of the Computer Science Department, and Libby Shoop and Ernest Retzel at the Computational Biology Centers, who have all contributed interesting ideas and discussions. I thank Dr. Gordon Legge of the Psychology Department, who introduced me to visual perceptual psychology. I thank my collegues at the User Interface Research Group for the camaraderie and foosball (Jeff Heer, Pam Schraedley, Julie Heiser, Christiaan Royer, Yuki Abe, Lichan Hong, Jock Mackinlay).

I would not have had the strength to complete this work during my graduate school years without the love of my big sister, Susan, and my great friends, Chad Juncker, Brook Kabanuk, Ahna Girshick, and Cate Gandrud. I thank my close circle of friends for their ability to deal with me during social settings and workouts (Adam Rosien, Jim Pitkow, Mark Waller, Ameeta Madhava, Members of the Stanford TaeKwonDo Program, Tim Ghormley). I thank my family (Dad Charles, Mom Sophia, Brother Tim, Nephews Alex and Brandon) for their continual support.

Writing this monograph has been like climbing a mountain, and the ups and the downs of its various stages is impossible to endure without support from family and friends. I am forever grateful of their belief in me.

Foreword

Much has been made over the power of the visual computer to let the eyes do some of the mind's work. Over the last fifteen years, it has become possible to compute real-time, animating images of mesmerizing beauty, images that unveil the essential order underlying a tangle of data. Visualization has been hailed as a new observational scientific instrument, kind of an electron microscope for data.

Actually, visualization should be thought of more as a tool, like a microtome for slicing data or a reagent for precipitating out its structure. Thinking of visualizations as insightful pictures leaves out the important role of manipulation, of operations done to the data in order to tease out yet other revealing images. Think of a neurologist choosing a Golgi stain to reveal pictures of the nodes of Ranier in a neural myelin sheath. Think of a scholar deftly twisting pictures of the literature this way and that to extract important connections and organize her paper. Interactive visualization gives the user not only an eye for data, but also an opposable thumb.

That is the aspiration, but present reality is less. Visualizations are hard enough to invent as visual representations. To get the full power of an idea, it has to be programmed from scratch, possibly over months. Faster to build are visualizations that can be stuck together from modules of a commercial visualization package. But these drastically reduce what can be done. Both of these methods are still too expensive to be part of the ongoing flow of an analysis. Some feeling of what it would be like to use visualization to explore an information space briskly comes from the technique of dynamic queries: Parametric adjustments to selection criteria on the data via sliders are instantly reflected in the display. With this technique, it is possible to discover sensitive points by wiggling the sliders and watching the visualization change. But dynamic queries work for pre-specified parameter adjustments. They are not nearly flexible enough for a wide-ranging sensemaking expedition.

What we are really talking about here is how a user can create operators of manipulation relevant to her problem quickly enough to be part of a flow of investigation. Full programming makes the widest set of operators possible, but even for those few users that can do it, the time cost is too great. Faster solutions are too limited. There are, however, examples of systems that can give users the sort of power that is needed. Emacs is one. Spreadsheets are another. Both are built off a set of operators that are combinatoric (that is, they can be combined in many ways) and involutional (that is, their outputs can be inputs for the other operators).

This brings us to the current book. Ed Chi's monograph works out these ideas in detail. He carefully chooses a set of combinatoric operators. This means that he has to disentangle operators on the data side from those on the visual side from those mapping between the two domains. He then creates an analogue to spreadsheet formulas and cells. Cells in his system can contain visualizations linked to other visualizations through references in the cell formulas. The result is an architecture in which a wide range of ad hoc analyses, based on preprogrammed components, can be done quickly. He shows that the architecture is general, by applying it to three very different domains. In short, he opens up a new paradigm for information visualization by showing that a data manipulation and visualization defining strategy based on spreadsheets does, in fact, work.

This is a significant achievement, because it shows how to break through one of the hard barriers in the use of computing and visualization. With only the level of time and effort characteristic of using a spreadsheet, the user can create sets of related visualizations. Furthermore, as a case study, the analysis of visual and data analysis into operators is exemplary for how other problems could be attacked.

I am happy that this work is finally being published in book form, so that it can have more opportunity to influence other work in the field. Chi has shown us all how visualization can be done using the eyes, but also using the hands.

Stuart K. Card, Research Fellow
Palo Alto Research Center
Feb. 1, 2001

Abstract

Information has become interactive. Information visualization is the design and creation of interactive graphic depictions of information by combining principles in the disciplines of graphic design, cognitive science, and interactive computer graphics. As the volume and complexity of the data increases, users require more powerful visualization tools that allow them to more effectively explore large abstract data sets.

Information visualization has traditionally been difficult to devise for each specific data set because of a number of issues. First, simply getting the data into the system is difficult. Data conversation and import issues have always plagued data analysts. Second, the domain-specific operations that are required in the analysis span a large range of possibilities. The operations could be specific data computational techniques such as statistical computing algorithms like clustering or correlation, or specific graphical analytical techniques such as using a spiral to represent time in order to examine the periodicity in the time series. Third, integration of domain-specific operators into an existing visualization system is difficult because most systems are not flexible or extensible enough to handle the integration easily.

Given these difficulties, this book has two goals:

(a) It seeks to make information visualization systems easier to develop by the creation of an information visualization framework. The complexity of operations and interactions requires a visualization framework that is easily understandable to both end-users and visualization designers. This book develops and discusses the general utility of a novel visualization reference model called *Data State Model*, and validates the model by applying it to various visualization techniques and showing several systems that illustrate how the model can be applied to make system-building easier.

(b) It applies this reference model to make information visualization more accessible to potential users by creating a "Visualization Spreadsheet", where each cell can contain an entire set of data represented using interactive graphics. The Visualization Spreadsheet embodies many of the concept in the Data State Model, and it serves as an example of the power of the visualization framework presented. Just as a numeric spreadsheet enables exploration of numbers, a visualization spreadsheet enables exploration of visual forms of information. Unlike numeric spreadsheets, which store only simple data elements and formulas in each cell, a cell in the Visualization Spreadsheet can hold an entire abstract data set, selection criteria, viewing specifications, and other information needed for a full-fledged information visualization. Similarly, intra-cell and inter-cell operations are far more complex, stretching beyond simple arithmetic and string operations to encompass a range of domain-specific operators.

We show that the spreadsheet and the Date State approach facilitates certain user tasks that are more difficult using other approaches. The Visualization Reference Model presented allows domain experts to define new data types and data operations, and enables visualization experts to incorporate new visualizations, viewing parameters, and view operations.

Whereas before one had to understand the intricacy of computer graphics in order to create interactive pictures representing data, this book seeks to make sophisticated pictorial techniques available to ordinary computer user.

Keywords: Information Visualization, Visualization, Visualization Framework, Visualization Model, Interactive Graphics, Visualization Systems, User Interface, User Interactions, Spreadsheet, Operators, View/value, Data State Model, Date Flow Model, Visualization Design, Application Extensibility, Sensemaking, Biological Sequence Analysis, Algorithm Visualization, World-Wide Web, Content Usage Structure Analysis, Information Ecologies.

Chapter 1

INTRODUCTION

A graphic is not "drawn" once and for all; it is "constructed" and reconstructed until it reveals all the relationships constituted by the interplay of the data.... A graphic is never an end in itself; it is a moment in the process of decision-making.

—Jacques Bertin [15, p. 16]

1. Motivation

We live in an exciting time. Great discoveries in science seem to come almost monthly, due in part to the proliferation of technology that helps scientists observe and explore more easily. It is now realistic to believe that, within our lifetimes, scientists may unlock the genetic code, better understand the working of the brain, and cure diseases that plague us. More powerful computer systems contribute to this rapid advance. The progression of computer technology is dramatic, and seemingly unending. The progression of computing tools, however, is helical, with feedback from each generation of tools used to motivate and specify the next generation. We are embarked on a new cycle of the helix, leading to a powerful tool we call "**Information Visualization**".

As computer scientists, we have been working with users in several different fields to build tools that help them see and learn. Problem-solving and decision-making are essential components of most complex tasks and are increasingly supported through novel user interfaces to information [67]. As the volume and complexity of information increases, users will need more powerful exploratory tools to effectively analyze the available information.

Our research is based on the techniques developed in the field of *Visualization*, which, put simply, is the use of visual representations of data sets to support understanding and analysis. Visualization techniques are capable of visually communicating vast amounts of information very quickly, and supports scientists and information analysts as they attempt to find meaning in large data sets. Interest in visualization-based user interfaces has blossomed in the past few years, with systems developed for applications from computational fluid dynamics [82] to geology [64], molecular biology [81, 31, 32], architectural plans [61], and animal behaviors [85].

Traditional *scientific visualizations* derive their graphical views based on the spatial representations inherent in the data. For example, earth geological information have spatial dimensions as part of the data set. In scientific visualization, these spatial dimensions are usually used as the basis of a visual map.

The field of *information visualization* has emerged as researchers seek ways to support understanding and analysis of *abstract data* through the use of interactive computer graphics and visualization techniques [25, 40, 23, 36, 110]. Abstract data is data that is not inherently geometric. In our daily lives, newspapers and magazines often employ graphical design principles to communicate simple statistical information, such as stock market financial data. There are a wealth of abstract information that has no physical spatial properties, such as document linkage structures, document similarity data. These abstract information present further challenges to visualization researchers because casting abstract data into effective visual forms is non-obvious. Indeed, research shows that the approach to graphic presentation can hinder or promote accurate and effective processing of information [101]. For this reason, researchers in information visualization have concentrated on semiology [15, 33]—the use of symbols and signs to communicate information.

However, in decision-making [15] and sensemaking [88], useful information is often derived from interacting and operating on the information with a variety of processing mechanisms [15, 25]. In particular, recent advances in information visualization interfaces have shown that visual analyses benefit not just from good visual representation methods, but also good interactions with those representations [2, 33, 102, 25]. These interfaces allow users to perform data analysis operations directly on the visual representation in order to see the effects.

In a visualization system, a set of well-designed interactions or *operators* can be used to answer a wide variety of questions. The design of a good set of visualization interactions requires domain-specific knowledge, since the problems of information analysis are grounded in the needs of a discipline. Because of the wide variety of data domains, the challenge is to design an single environment that enables users to perform a variety of difficult visualization tasks in an intuitive manner. Fortunately, although different domain applications often require different visual representations, many of these domains share similar view manipulations or data transformation operations.

By developing and employing a conceptual model for visualization, we can analyze and categorize the similarities between these data domains. Without such a model, the differences among these domains threaten to prohibit the sharing of similar operations. In this book, we use this model to take advantage of the similarities between the operations among different data domains. In doing so, we enable users to perform a wide variety of information analysis tasks. For example, it is useful to have visualizations for related data sets displayed simultaneously side-by-side. Furthermore, there are a number of operations that one would want to apply to the visualizations simultaneously, such as comparing and filtering multiple data sets simultaneously. By enabling users to perform tasks under the same conceptual model, more analysis tasks could be accomplished by the same visualization interface.

The challenge, therefore, is to develop a system with an intuitive user interface that can accomodate the task requirements of a wide variety of visualization domains and enable users to easily operate on related data sets in the system in a coordinated way. In the past, researchers have examined the use of data flow charts. Data flow network visualization systems have shown that it is an effective way to construct scientific visualizations [98, 103, 43, 54, 8, 50].

We examine an alternative user interface model called Data State Model. In a Data Flow system, the focus is on *how to specify* to the computer the various steps that are needed to perform a specific analysis. Here the focus of the model is on the *process* of visualization. By contrast, in a Data State system, the focus is on the various *stages of data*. The idea is that, if we visualize all of the intermediate steps of the visualization, the user can interactively explore the potential of any number of processes that can be applied to generate a new state of the data. The focus here is on exploring the data *states* that are possible.

To better explore this idea, let us first examine the cognitive processes used during analysis of data.

2. Cognitive Advantages of the Information Visualization

In this section, we first establish some background on the cognitive advantages of information visualization. In particular, we review visual information processing, and a cognitive science analysis of task structures called "sense-making". Then we explain how information visualization and the models and systems described in this book supports visual sensemaking.

2.1 Visual Information Processing

In the present and the past, knowledge workers have utilized various technologies to reduce the cost of accessing, processing, and understanding large data sets. The vision of Vannevar Bush's 'MEMEX' was to enable workers to make sense of information by employing technology that allow them to "make real use of the record" [22] by extracting relationships between pieces of information.

Even though people are inherently drawn to elegant graphics, the use of abstract symbols in statistical graphics to represent information did not develop until late 18th century. William Playfair (1759–1823) almost single handedly invented and improved upon nearly all fundamental graphical designs used in statistical graphics [101]—length and area to show quantity, scatterplots, bar charts, line plots. The use of statistical graphics to show numbers has since become a fixture in communicating information in our daily lives in printed forms of newspapers and magazines [101]. *Information Visualization* as a technology has extended our capability for communicating immense amounts of both real and abstract information [25].

In *visual information processing*, our visual, perceptual, and cognitive abilities enhance our problem-solving skills. Visual metaphors are even used for information understanding [25]: gaining an understanding of a concept is often called "seeing", reducing a problem into its essentials is called "focusing", uncovering a problem is called "bringing to light". Clearly, our ability to see and decipher relies heavily on our perceptual and cognitive abilities [25].

2.2 Sensemaking Cycle and Information Ecology

Cognitive psychologists have developed frameworks to model how we use our perceptual and cognitive abilities to absorb information. A popular model is called the "*sensemaking model*" [88]. Sensemaking is a term that describes the cognitive process in bringing new light on knowledge. There is an extensive analysis of sensemaking tasks, which is found to be cyclic and iterative [88, 15].

As an example, consider the task of conducting a literature survey on infectivity factors of retroviruses in a physical library. Trained librarians have a set of processing tools that provides information on the choice of next step, such as the author or keyword searches, citation indices, encyclopedias, dictionaries, and bibliographies. With these tools, librarians can accomplish many tasks. Continuing with the example, an overview article is first selected. Then its bibliography is consulted to pick out a list of other related articles that fits the user's interest profile. Next, the user returns to the stacks of the library to collect these papers, and the cycle repeats until the user is satisfied with the literature survey.

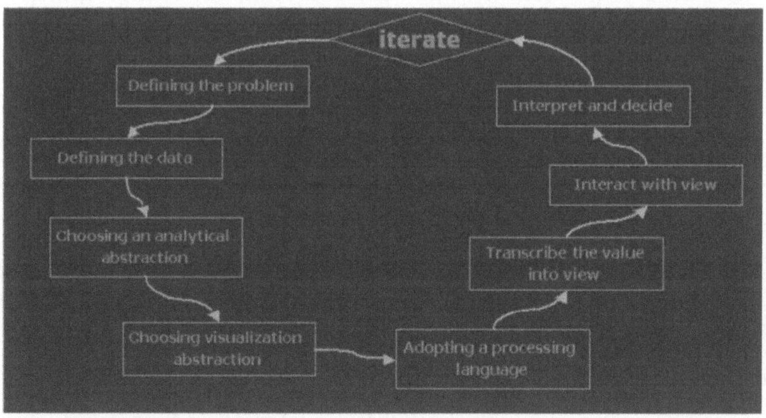

Figure 1.1. This figure depicts the Visual Sensemaking Cycle, and the various steps that are required to create a full analysis system.

The library is an example of a type of information environment, and has been the primary source of information for many centuries. New types of information environment have been developing since the invention of the digital computer. The World-

Wide Web is quickly acquiring a large user community, and becoming the primary source of information for many information tasks [57]. Cognitive psychologists have described this rich relationship between users and an information environment as an *inxinformation ecology* [78, 79]. The word "ecology" is used to describe how the task and/or the information changes and evolves through time. People seek information and consume it in these information ecologies, and they form strategies for acquiring the most important pieces of information.

Psychologists have observed that information access environments needs to support the sensemaking process by offering tools that enable cyclic task structures [88, 15, 78]. Each cycle during sensemaking gains new knowledge about the information.

2.3 Levels of Knowledge

The aim in the sensemaking cycle is to successively discover new higher-level knowledge about the information [88, 15, 28]. This requires the uncovering of new relationships between information elements, or subsets. This means we must support ways of constructing new groupings of data defined by the interplay of relationships between elements.

1 Elementary or Local Level: This is equivalent to finding a specific entry in the data model. It is important that visualization tools always provide access to the precise values at this level using detail-on-demand, e.g. what was the access frequency of http://www.xerox.com/index.html?

2 Intermediate or Comparison Level: Information at this level consists of relationships that exist between subsets of information, e.g. are access patterns in May 1998 comparable to a year ago?

3 Overall or Global Level: This is the highest level attainable from the data. The knowledge obtained at this level is condensed from the correlation between one variable of the data with another variable, e.g. are there any usage trends governed by time in the data set?

The discussion of different levels of knowledge would not be complete unless we also discuss the various ways in which different levels of knowledge can be reached. The key ingredient in tying all of this together is a formal analysis of the *operators* that would take us from one level of knowledge to another level. This is one of the many purposes of the Data State Model.

Some examples of the kind of operators we are thinking of include mathematical analysis algorithms. Mathematical analysis of the problem can often provide glimpse of higher level information, but requires visualization to make sense of the patterns [15]. A simple example would be the computation of averages and confidence intervals of groups of numeric data. We often use a scatter plot with error bars to make sense of this statistical analysis.

A more sophisticated example is Spreading Activation [4], which is an algorithm for computing the relevance between items. Anderson and Pirolli developed Spreading Activation in 1984 to model the way human memory gets activated to provide relevant information to a cognitive task. They showed that this algorithm can be effectively used to predict the relevance of a piece of information in the context of a task. Spreading activation can be computed using various pieces of information, such as structure of the links and frequency of usage, co-citation strength between documents, and word-vector based similarity [79]. Spreading activation provides information at the intermediate level by condensing the relationship between each node and its relevance to all other documents in the set.

We will discuss how these operators fit into the framework of a visualization system.

2.4 System Requirements of Visual Sensemaking

From a cognitive point of view, the potential success of information visualization eliminates many of the stumbling blocks in information analysis and data processing because the information visualization may:

- Form an external cognition device. In using the information visualization, the user constructs the required information in each step of the analysis. Step by step, the user forms an understanding of the relationship between the pieces of information. What is needed is a way to show intermediate results as this process unfolds. By externalizing this cognition process of sensemaking and by showing the intermediate results of each operation, an information visualization system becomes an externalized cognition device.

- Reduce the cost-structure of the analysis. Information visualization systems in any doman should allow new, ad hoc analyses to be defined quickly. Instead of the cost of programming new analyses in each new situation, the system should allow a wide-range of new analyses to be defined as combination of other past analyses. By structuring a few simple rules for applying operations, the user may readily apply processing mechanisms very quickly.

- Enables continuous iterative exploratory data analysis. As users find new knowledge in their data, they can quickly formulate new directions for data discoveries by re-tailoring the system. If we can enable this, creative insights congeal because the analysis cycle can continue uninterrupted. During analysis, the information visualization system should enable users to operate the system at about the same pace as the users' cognitive deductions.

- Identifies new operators to add to the analysis repertoire. Our Data State Model framework gives domain experts the ability to analyze the structure of the data and their associated analytical abstractions. During this process, new operators are identified by the analysts, and this increases the modularity and flexibility of the system.

3. Data State Model and the Visualization Spreadsheet Supports Visual Sensemaking

The question before us is then: "How to design a system that utilizes the Data State Model so that it appropriately supports visual sensemaking?"

Using the Data State Model and to illustrate its differences from past visualization systems, our idea is to build a *Visualization Spreadsheet*, which is a spreadsheet-like interactive program enabling a user to lay out data on the screen in rows and columns of cells, where the cells contain data sets that are viewed through visualization. Each cell enables the user to view the data *states* in the analysis during intermediate stages.

So the second goal of the book is to illustrate the Visualization Spreadsheet, a system built using the Data State Model. The Visualization Spreadsheet supports complex data exploration where many parameters of a data set, or a group of data sets, are explored in a coordinated way. Our research seeks to create a Visualization Spreadsheet that is as intuitive as a numeric spreadsheet such as Microsoft Excel, but instead of numbers, each cell can display an entire set of data represented using interactive graphics.

The spreadsheet metaphor provides a structured, intuitive, and powerful interface for exploratory data analysis. Spreadsheets have proven to be highly successful environments for interacting with numeric data by providing an environment that easily affords the application and reapplication of a variety of data analysis operations. Since computer users are accustom to the spreadsheet metaphor, we expect user skills in numerical spreadsheets to transfer easily to the Visualization Spreadsheet. The wide variety of operators and their complexity may thwart this transfer.

The challenge is to design a intuitive interface for this wide array of operators. We examine both command languages and direct manipulation interfaces in an attempt to understand how these two techniques can be used in a spreadsheet interface. Numerical spreadsheets map operators to textual commands to partially solve this problem. We examine both textual and direct manipulation operators in the context of the Data State Model and show how it can effectively model all of these visualization operators.

4. Visualization Spreadsheet Defined

The concept of the Visualization Spreadsheet is based on four characteristics—visualization in cells, grid layout, operators, and dependency. These properties gives the Visualization Spreadsheet its characteristics. Many of these characteristics it shares with traditional numeric spreadsheets.

- **Visualization in Cells**. The Visualization Spreadsheet displays the visualization of an arbitrarily large data set in each cell. Cells are adapted to handle large datasets instead of a few numbers. They handle visual representations of complex data-types with text strings, hierarchical structures, and regular and irregular shapes. Because spreadsheets now contain groups of large datasets, users can now see much more than just a single dataset in an established context.

- **Grid layout**. The grid layout lets users view collections of visualizations simultaneously. The tabular layout has proven useful in numeric spreadsheets, and has a number of advantages. First, it enables users to enter data into cells in various configurations. Second, because of its easy-to-comprehend structure, the cells are easy to navigate to and from. Third, because it affords easy grouping, operations can be defined on rows and columns, or portions of a spreadsheet.

- **Operators**. Operators are available for generating or modifying cell contents. Since the datasets are no longer just simple numbers, the operations now consist a variety of operators for different types of datasets. This also results in more difficulties in the design of the user interface for these operations. Operators can be applied across a specified range of operand cells, such as an entire column or row. Certain operators may take columns, rows, or a subgroup of cells as operands.

- **Dependency**. Just as in traditional numeric spreadsheets, the data in a cell can be computed from the data in other cells, because cells may contain references to other datasets in other cells. The spreadsheet keeps track of the dependencies between cells and automatically updates the cells appropriately when they are manipulated. A cell's data is recalculated automatically whenever a data on which it depends changes.

5. Overview

In summary, in this book we develope a novel information visualization conceptual model called the "Data State Model" that helps end-users, visualization analysts, and designers. We show how our model describes a wide variety of information visualization techniques. This model undertaken in this project allows domain experts to define new data types and data operations and enables visualization experts to incorporate new visualizations, viewing parameters, and view operations. We extend existing information visualization reference models and show how it applies to general information visualization problems.

Also in this book, we use this new development in the model to build a new system called the Visualization Spreadsheet. We show that the Visualization Spreadsheet is a powerful environment that enables users to more effectively explore available information. Computer users care about such a tool since it will help them interpret information and enable exploration tasks that were previously impossible. We designed, implemented, and evaluated a general visualization spreadsheet framework that is applicable for many kinds of data. The contribution of this project are: (1) Understanding of when and how the Visualization Spreadsheet can be applied, (2) Understanding of what user tasks are particularly suitable for the spreadsheet, and (3) Understanding of a general visualization conceptual model that can be tailored to multiple data domains and data analysis situations.

The remainder of this book is structured as follows. In Chapter 8, we describe past and present research in fields related to the two goals of this book. In Chapter 2, we define and describe the Data State Model, which is the visualization framework we used in the implementation. We describe the interesting properties of our framework, as well as how it can be used to classify visualization operators.

In Chapter 4, we describe the relationship between the Data State Model framework and the Data Flow Model used in traditional data flow visualization systems. In particular, we show that the two have equivalent expressive power in describing visualizations, but each have their merits. In Chapter 3, we further validate our framework by classifying the operators in a large number of visualization techniques using the Data State Model.

In Chapter 5, we discuss the Visualization Spreadsheet and its case studies and task scenarios. We analyze the advantages of the Visualization Spreadsheet concept and abstract them into a set of principles. The case studies include several interesting data domains, such as molecular biology sequence analysis, time-series matrices, and algorithm visualization. In Chapter 6, we include a detailed case study of the Visualization Spreadsheet on the analysis of content, usage, and structure of a large World-Wide Web site. In Chapter 7, we mention how our visualization spreadsheet systems are implemented, and describe their architectures. We also discuss some of the implementation issued and lessons learned during implementation. Chapter 9 contains concluding remarks.

Chapter 2

DATA STATE REFERENCE MODEL

In a much larger study ..., the construction of the table depends not only on the data but especially on the hypotheses and the available means for reducing these data. These means are the mathematical and graphical methods of information-processing.

—Jacques Bertin [15, p. 17]

Information visualization encounters a wide variety of different data domains. The visualization community has developed many different representation methods and interactive techniques. As a community, we have realized that the requirements in each domain are often dramatically different. In order to understand, classify, and easily apply existing graphical representation methods in separate domains, researchers have developed a taxonomy and semiology of graphic representations methods [14, 25, 24, 101]. A major difference between current information visualization work and past work on graphic design is the development of interactivity. The dialog between human and computer enriches the communication of information.

Therefore, we seek to further develop a reference framework for visualization operators and interactions in visualization systems. We will then use this framework in the visualization spreadsheet. We discuss properties of this framework and use it to characterize operations spanning a variety of different visualization techniques. The model developed here enables a new way of exploring and evaluating the design space of visualization operators, and helps end-users in their analysis tasks.

1. The Need for a Reference Model for Operations

Imagine a visualization application with two views of the same source data set, say a HomeFinder application [2]. In this application, the user is to find a potential home to purchase using a number of criteria, such as the number of bedrooms, geographical location, price, etc. The user seeks potential homes by filtering out homes that do not satisfy the her list of desirable features. Imagine that in one view, the data set is visualized using a scatter plot display with dynamic query sliders [2], while the other view shows the values using a sorted numeric table.

Now let's use the sliders to filter out some data points. The scatter plot view changes accordingly. However, a question of semantics arises for the table view. One possible interpretation of this action is that the table view is a totally independent view of the original data set, and therefore should not change its view. The other possible interpretation is that the original data source is being modified by this interaction, which means the table view should change accordingly! Which of these two possibilities is the correct interpretation?

Let's try to solve this problem of contradictory semantics by examining the application domain. Assume the user is interested in selecting homes in a relatively expensive neighborhood that fall in her price range. Say that the user is interested in seeing the distribution of the homes over the geographical locations while she manipulates the price slider to include only highly-priced homes. If the user is merely interested in how the plot view changes while manipulating the price sliders, we would then argue that the table view should not change at all, because the task semantics do not require the original data source to be modified. If the user is actually interested in *creating a new data set* that only contains homes in her price range, then we would argue that the original data set is indeed being *modified*, and therefore the table view should change accordingly. Both interpretations of the interaction are valid under this task scenario! The user needs a "Do What I Mean" key that requests the behavior she intends.

1.1 Problems from End-Users' Perspective

The above example shows that end-users often have difficulty interacting with visualization systems because there is a wide *gulf of execution*—"a difference between the intentions and the allowable possible actions" [74]. Sometimes the semantics of operations are imprecise, or worse, impossible to achieve. The user is often left with no way of predicting the result of her actions, or may even be incapable of selecting the operation she desires from among several alternatives.

The gulf of execution is evidence that the operation and interaction model of a visualization system often hampers the analysis process because it does not fulfill the needs of the analysis. We can construct similar scenarios by examining other data domains, such as visualizing hierarchical structures like file systems or organizational charts, slices of a 3D human brain, or world-wide web linkage structures. Fundamentally, each of these data domains have data and its associated visualized view, therefore filtering actions in these data domains will also have the same exact ambiguous meanings. So this problem exists even after careful consideration of the application task domain.

The HomeFinder example emphasizes the difference between view and value. The *value* of a visualization is the raw data set being visualized. The *view* controls the way that this raw data is represented on the screen. In information visualization, since the data is represented abstractly on the screen, there is a distinct separation between the value of the data and the view of the data, and it is especially useful to represent the same data in many different ways. This is different from other areas of visualization, such as fluid dynamics or volume visualization, where there is a tighter coupling between the value of the data and its visual representation. In HomeFinder, the user needs the ability to decouple the view and the value, so that they can be specified and changed independently. We call this *View/Value Separation*.

View/Value separation is not a property that existing visualization reference models capture in their understanding of operators, leaving users with the difficult task of figuring out how to operate on view and value separately, if this is at all possible. New visualization models are needed that bridge this gulf of execution by presenting a consistent visualization model that not only is valid in one application domain, but is also valid across several application domains. This consistency is especially important in visualization systems that tailor to multiple data domains, because users will be able to transfer their knowledge of the usage of visualization applications across domains based on a consistent user mental model.

1.2 Problems from Designers' Perspective

Visualization designers face problems that are similar to ones that end-users face. They need to provide a user model and deal with view/value separation and its semantic issues. An additional issue faced by designers daily is how to flexibly extend a visualization system to include new data domains.

1.2.1 Providing a User Model

One approach to solving the view/value separation issue is to think about how value is turned into a view. In scientific visualization, past work in data flow networks and the visualization pipeline helped users to focus on the visualization process. Because these models were designed with the goal of providing a processing model, they have enabled designers and end-users to better understand how operators interact with each other. We seek to develop a model that makes use of the concepts in the visualization pipeline to help designers present user models that are consistent with possible user intentions. Such a model could help us eliminate errors caused by imprecise or incorrect conceptual models, and potentially bridge the *gulf of evaluation*—the feedback from the system is "directly interpretable in terms of the intentions and expectations of the person" [74]. In other words, the model must help users in evaluating and performing the actions appropriate to the task.

Another issue in user models is that, in different problem-solving situations, users prefer to focus variously on the operations to achieve a single desired result, or on the operands at various stages in the computation. As an example of an *operation focus* model, the traditional visualization pipeline model focuses on the *process* of the visualization, rather than on the *state* of the data. The user interface of such a system generally consist of a diagram editor that allows users to drag-and-drop processing modules onto a canvas and connect them with data pipes. As an example of a *data state focus*, in commercial numeric spreadsheets such as Microsoft Excel, instead of showing the explicit relationships between variables (the numeric equations), the system hides those relationships in favor of showing the operands of the formulas. This enables the user to focus on the intermediate computational results. For this reason, commercial numeric spreadsheets emphasize the operands.

Instead of focusing on the process, sometimes the user is more concerned with the state of her data. This mode of interaction is especially useful in situations where the next analysis step is not immediately apparent. By showing the state of the data, the user gets visual feedback that helps bridge the gulf of evaluation. The user can evaluate the result of her last action and choose the next step based on the results of the computation. Therefore, in addition to describing the analysis process, we seek a user model that allows us to capture the data states so we can accurately provide feedback and support these exploratory interactions. We call this *data state focus*. We need a model that not only describes the data transformation process such as the visualization pipeline, but that also models the data states.

1.2.2 Extensibility to New Data Domains

In designing a generalized visualization system, we will encounter many new data domains. In extending a visualization system to include a new data domain, the first step is often requirements analysis. The result of requirements analysis is often a user study that specifies the groupings of user tasks or operations, but visualization designers have no framework in which to take advantage of these analyses. From these requirements analysis, designers often have no idea how to start designing, classifying, and specifying the influences between a set of operators and interactions. While information visualization has made great strides in the development of a semiology of graphical representation methods [14, 65, 24], we still lacks a comprehensive framework for studying visualization operations.

Consider our proposal for a Visualization Spreadsheet [30], for example. Spreadsheet environments are powerful because of a rich set of operators. One of the challenges of applying a spreadsheet to information visualization is the wide variety of data domains that are dealt with in information visualization. Therefore, the flexibility and the generalizability of the spreadsheet hinge on the application programmers' ability to extend the spreadsheet with additional operators as needed for their application domain.

However, the disparities between different types of operators and their applicability in different situations make operators difficult to implement and reuse. The development of a visualization model that can handle these dispartities is crucial.

1.3 Reference Model Helps Users and Designers

So from the viewpoint of end-users and designers, we see that there is a need to construct a general reference model—a conceptual model that enables us to clearly classify and organize different operators. An *operator framework* is a conceptual model for all possible visualization operations. By *operation*, we mean all user interactions, whether based on direct manipulation or other interaction. A *visualization reference model* helps visualization designers describe the data processing process, focus on the data states, and form an operator framework for all of the visualization operations that are possible in the system.

Our motivation can be distilled into three major goals. First, we need to develop a framework that is sufficiently clean and simple that it enables end-users to choose which operator to apply for a desired result. Second, we need the model to help the end-user to predict the results of their interactions with the visualization system. The biggest benefit of achieving these two goals is establishing a user conceptual model that allows us to bridge the conceptual gulf of execution and evaluation for the end-user. Thirdly, we need to develop a general interaction model for information visualization that helps visualization designers classify and understand the relationships between operators and the composition of interactions. This model will enable us to organize operators by classifying and taxonomizing the space of possible operations.

Herb Simon once said in understanding any phenomenon, the first step is to "develop a taxonomy" [93]. The inherent value of classification and understanding is that it enables us to isolate the important artifacts for design. In information visualization, an operator framework will allow us to build interaction models for new data domains.

While we were motivated by our research in the Visualization Spreadsheet [30], these are general questions about the utility of visualization systems, because it is often unclear how domain-specific operators are to be integrated into visualization systems. Without the ability to incorporate domain-specific operators, a visualization toolkit or system would be useless. Furthermore, there are many operators that are not domain-specific but are not effectively reused in different applications. The framework must enable us to better understand the interaction between data, view, and the operators. We need an effective operator framework in order to better understand these issues. In summary, the operator framework should enable both end-users and designers to better understand the situations in which operators can be applied, how operators can be applied, and what operators do when they are applied.

2. Fundamental Properties of Operators

In order to develop an operator framework, we first start by observing some fundamental properties of operators. One property is whether an operator is a view or value operator—whether it modifies the underlying data set or not. The other property is degree of functional similarity with other operators. These two properties are important because functional similarity deals with an operator's degree of applicability, whereas the degree of View/Value Separation has deep implications regarding the semantics of the operator.

2.1 View versus Value

One dimension of operators is whether it is view-oriented or value-oriented. By **Value**, we mean the raw data, whereas **View** is the visualization end-product. A *Value Operator* changes the data source by such processes as adding or deleting subsets of the data, filtering or modifying the raw data, and performing a Fourier Transform on an image. A value operator fundamentally generates a new data set.

A *View Operator*, on the other hand, changes the visualization content only. Examples of such operators include 3D rotation, translation, and zooming, a horizontal or vertical flip of an image, and changing transparency values of a surface in order to see the underlying structures better. A view operator fundamentally does not change the underlying data set.

The distinction between a view and value operator is not always clear. For instance, for an image, since the value is the image pixel values, the modification of the colormap represents a raw pixel value modification, and therefore, should be classified as a value operator. However, in a 3D surface heat map, the modification of the heat color scale appears to be a view change that does not fundamentally change the underlying surface values. Another example is the HomeFinder [2] application in Section 1. Sometimes we would like to apply filtering to generate a data set. Other times we just like to temporarily make certain data points invisible without affecting the underlying data source. The same filtering operation appears to change its property depending on the user's intentions!

How do we unify such seemingly contradictory classification of operators according to this important property? View/value does not appear to be a black and white property for operators.

2.2 Operational versus Functional Similarity

In developing our model, we observed that some operators are **operationally similar** across applications—operations whose underlying implementations are exactly the same from application to application. Some examples of such operations include rotations, scaling, translation, camera position manipulation, geometric object manipulation, and lighting. The entire class of geometric and scene operators are operationally similar across applications, because we can make a fundamental assumption that once we obtain a view, we are dealing with graphic primitives such as lines and polygons. We can operate on these lines and polygons without regard to its original data sources. There are other operators that belong in this class, such as duplicating or deleting a view or value, and renaming a data source.

We also observed that there are operators that are only **functionally similar**—operations that are semantically similar across applications, but the underlying code implementations are different for different types of data sets. For example, filtering a data set is a common and extremely useful operation, but different application domains have different ways of filtering the data set, since each domain has very different data structures. Another example is the class of algebraic operators such as adding or subtracting data sets, which is again domain specific. The way we add two for-sale real estate property lists together is not the same as combining the Web linkage structures from two different crawls of the Web.

Finally, there are operators that are completely application task dependent. These are operations that are specially designed for a specific task in a particular application domain. An example of this class of operations is triggering a heart pulse by first inserting an electrical probe during a heart electrical pulse visualization. We could specify the positioning of a probe using the mouse. The electrical simulation process is a domain task-specific operation. Another example is a specific implementation of the hypertext document parsing operation, or multi-dimensional scaling for a document set, or computing similarity of documents.

The concepts of functional and operational similarity are related to the concepts of view and value operators. On the one hand, view operations tend to be more operationally similar across application domains. On the other hand, value operators tend to appear functionally similar but are implemented differently for each data domain. Even though there are classes of value operators, such as combining data sets, a value operator must operate on the specific data structures from the application domain. But view operators, such as scene, geometric, and pixel operations, operates on the displayed visualization end-product, which we can assume to be graphic primitives such as points, lines, polygons, or voxels. We need a model that fits with this observation.

3. A Reference Model for Visualization Operators

3.1 Visualization Pipeline

Our discovery is that the solution to the above dilemma comes from a non-intuitive source—the visualization pipeline. We developed a visualization operator framework [29] that places operators in the context of the information visualization pipeline [25]. Visualization operators operate on data as well as views. On one end of the pipeline, we have the raw data (value), while on the other end, we have the visualization (view).

We propose that the view/value property for operators is a fundamental classification for what stage the operator is in the visualization pipeline. On the one end of the spectrum, we have full view operators that can only be interpreted as view operators, such as rotation. On the other extreme, we have full value operators that can only be interpreted as value operators, such as expanding an existing data set by adding a new data set. Operators that are not full view or full value operators lie in between the two extremes. One example is the multi-dimensional scaling information processing technique, which reduces the dimensionality of data sets. Other examples of these types of operators include operators related to textual word frequency vectors, which are produced from a set of documents. For example, keyword clustering techniques can be applied to a wide variety of different types of documents, and can be shared among all data domains that are related to textual documents.

In this framework, value is converted and transformed into four major stages: Value, Analytical Abstraction, Visualization Abstraction, and View (see Table 2.1). In between each of these four stages, there are three major processing steps: Data Transformation, Visualization Transformation, and Visual Mapping Transformation (see Table 2.2).

Stage	Description
Value	The raw data.
Analytical Abstraction	Processed data that is not yet mappable but include all information from the raw data that will be visualized.
Visualization Abstraction	Information that is mappable and visualizable on the screen using at least one visualization technique.
View	The end-product of the visualization mapping, where the user sees and interprets the picture presented to her.

Table 2.1. Information Visualization Pipeline stages

Processing Steps	Description
Data Transformation	Generates some form of analytical abstraction from the value (usually by extraction).
Visualization Transformation	Takes an analytical abstraction and further reduce it into some form of visualization abstraction, which is visualizable content.
Visual Mapping Transformation	Takes information that is in a visualizable format and presents a graphical view to the user.

Table 2.2. Transformation Steps in InfoVis Pipeline

In information visualization, data domains usually contain complicated pipelines. For example, a model is shown in Figure 2.1, which is expanded from Stuart Card's information visualization model). Here we describe its *transformation steps*:

1 Raw data are first processed into some form of analytical abstraction, which are processed data that contain all the information to be visualized, through a *Data Transformation* process.

2 This analytical abstraction is often further reduced using a visualization transformation into some form of visualization abstraction, which is infor-

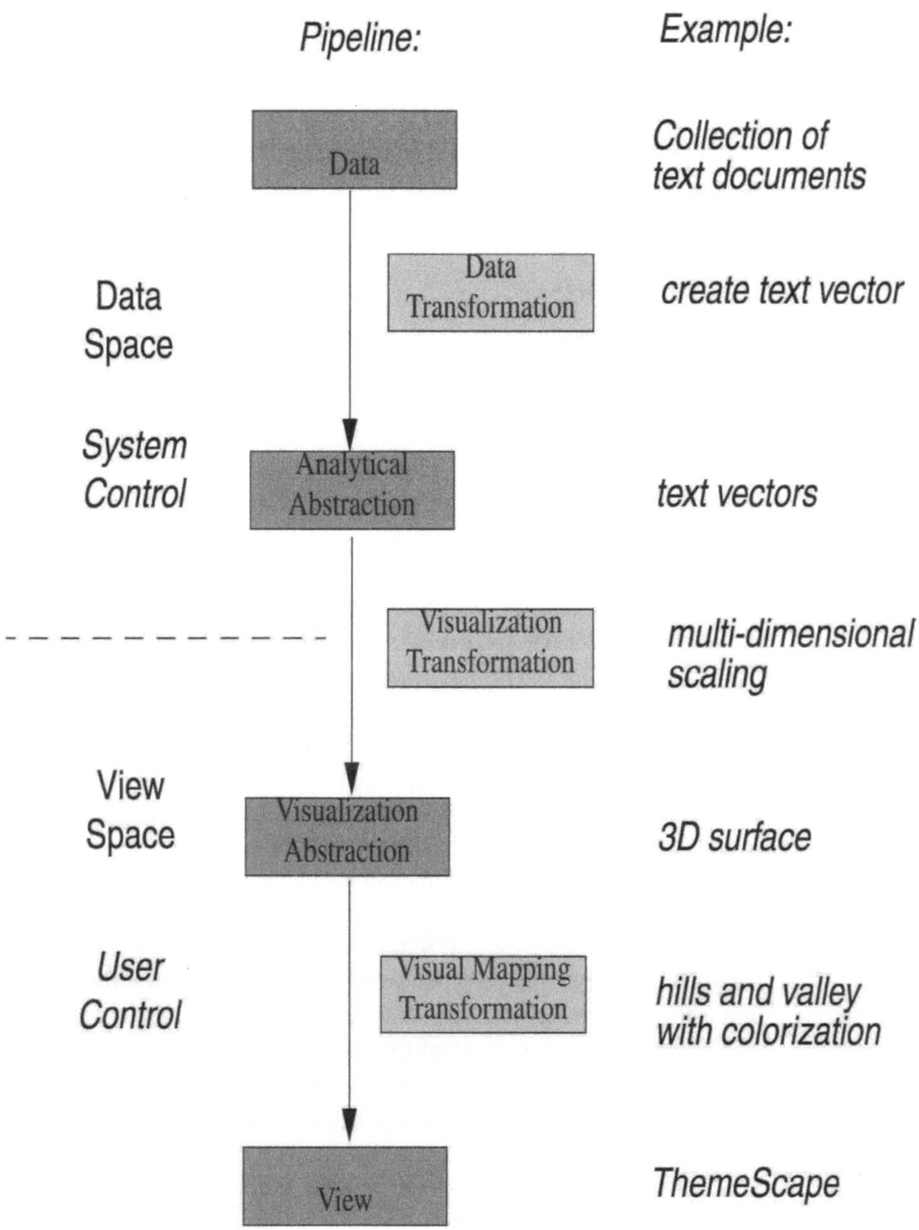

Figure 2.1. The Information Visualization Reference Model

mation content that is visualizable. Usually this process contains a dimension reduction step, because the data sets in information visualization are complex and multi-dimensional, and only a few dimensions can be projected or displayed on the screen at a time. An example of *Visualization Transformation* is multi-dimensional scaling and clustering.

3 From the visualization abstraction, there is a further step of *Visual Mapping Transformation* that brings a view that is presentable to the user on the computer display[1]

3.2 Data State Model

In order to accurately emphasize the end-user's analysis process as well as the intermediate results, we constructed a new model called the Data State Model based on the visualization pipeline. Figure 2.2 contains a depiction of the framework with example web analysis operators. The modifications are two-fold.

First, while the visualization pipeline handles a large variety of operators, the pipeline model does not take multiple values and multiple views into account. If two separate data sets go through two different pipelines to contribute to a single visualization, the model breaks down. In order to ameliorate this problem, we expand the pipeline into a network that allows as many values and as many views as needed. To this extent, our model is similar to data flow networks as presented in [92].

Second, the visualization pipeline uses nodes to represent operators, and edges to represent flow of data. The use of nodes to represent operators emphasizes the processing stages in the pipeline rather than the data states. This causes visualization pipeline models to omit the details of how individual data sets is processed. Instead, we use a state model, where each node represents a certain data state, and each edge is an operator transforming the data from one state to the next. Instead of stages, each node in the network is a state describing the status of the data. Each directed edge from a state to another state describes the operator that is applied to modify the data. The source data states are the raw values, whereas the sinks are the views of the data sets.

As an example, the visualization Data State Model used to construct a Delaunay Triangulation visualization example is shown in

[1]Most visual mapping transformations do not preserve the precision of the data in the visualization abstraction. Furthermore, computer graphics on a bitmapped display is inherently a discrete mapping, since there is only finite amount of pixels on the screen, and finite number of colors available. Other effects, such as occlusions, shadows, and lighting, can affect the perception of values.

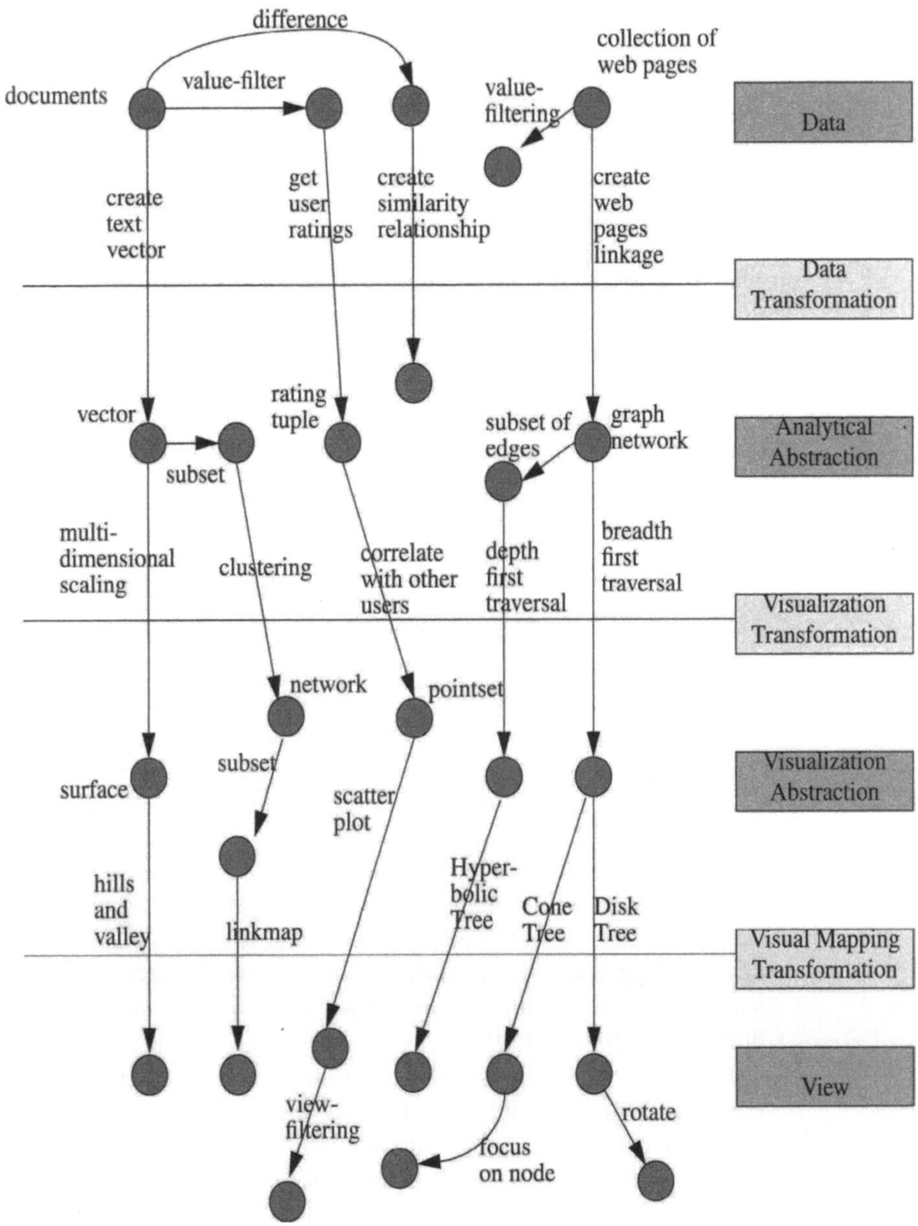

Figure 2.2. Our visualization operator framework: Data State Model

Figure 2.3. An example of the kind of visualization constructed by this model can be seen in Figure 5.5. It is an example of a simple Data State Model for generating a visualization. This example applies our framework to show how the Data State Model takes data sets and generates intermediate results and finally creates a visualized view of the data set.

Our example consists of a random number generator that takes a seed number to start its operation. Then using this random number generator, the "MathRandom3D" operator creates 3D point sets. Then the Delaunay Triangulation operator creates a tetrahedra collection, which is then transparently rendered into a visualization. The diagram shows that this same tetrahedra collection can also be edge rendered into a different visualization that only shows the edges. We can then apply different view operators to these visualizations to create new views. A different algorithm could have been applied to the point set to generate a Voronoi diagram, which can be rendered to create a different visualized view.

3.3 Example: Web Analysis in the Data State Model

Let's see an example of applying this framework to a specific application domain—visualization of Web sites. The pipeline that these operators are classified in is presented in Figure 2.4.

The raw data set is a collection of Web pages generated by crawling a Web site. We can first perform a value-filtering operator where we search for documents that contain the word "Hewlett-Packard" or "HP". This would be an example of *Within Data Stage Operator*, because the raw data has exactly the same data format, with simply a specific reduction in data set size. We can then use this collection of Web pages and generate a graph network (the analytical abstraction) from the linkages between pages. This is a data transformation operation, because the data format changed during this processing step.

Using the network, we can again select only subsets of the edges, such as choosing only the first three levels of documents from the root node. This subset operation is an example of a *Within Analytical Abstraction Stage Operator*. We can then create a tree by doing a breadth first traversal (a visualization transformation operation). The breadth first traversal generates a visualization abstraction, a hierarchical tree of the Web pages, that can be easily visualized. There are many visual mapping techniques that can be applied to this visualization abstraction, such as Cone Tree [87], Disk Tree [28], TreeMap [56], Hyperbolic Tree [59].

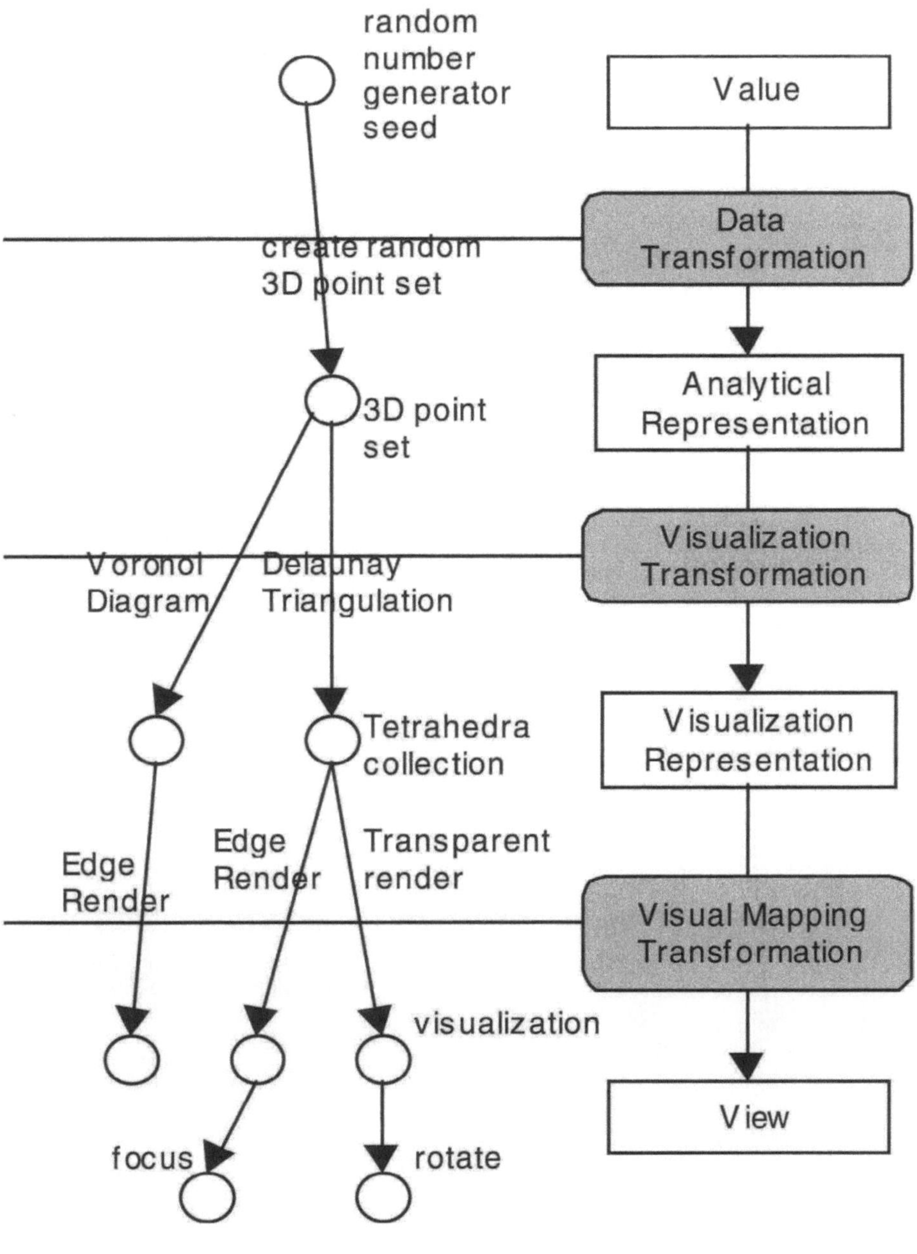

Figure 2.3. The Delaunay Triangulation Algorithm Visualization Pipeline

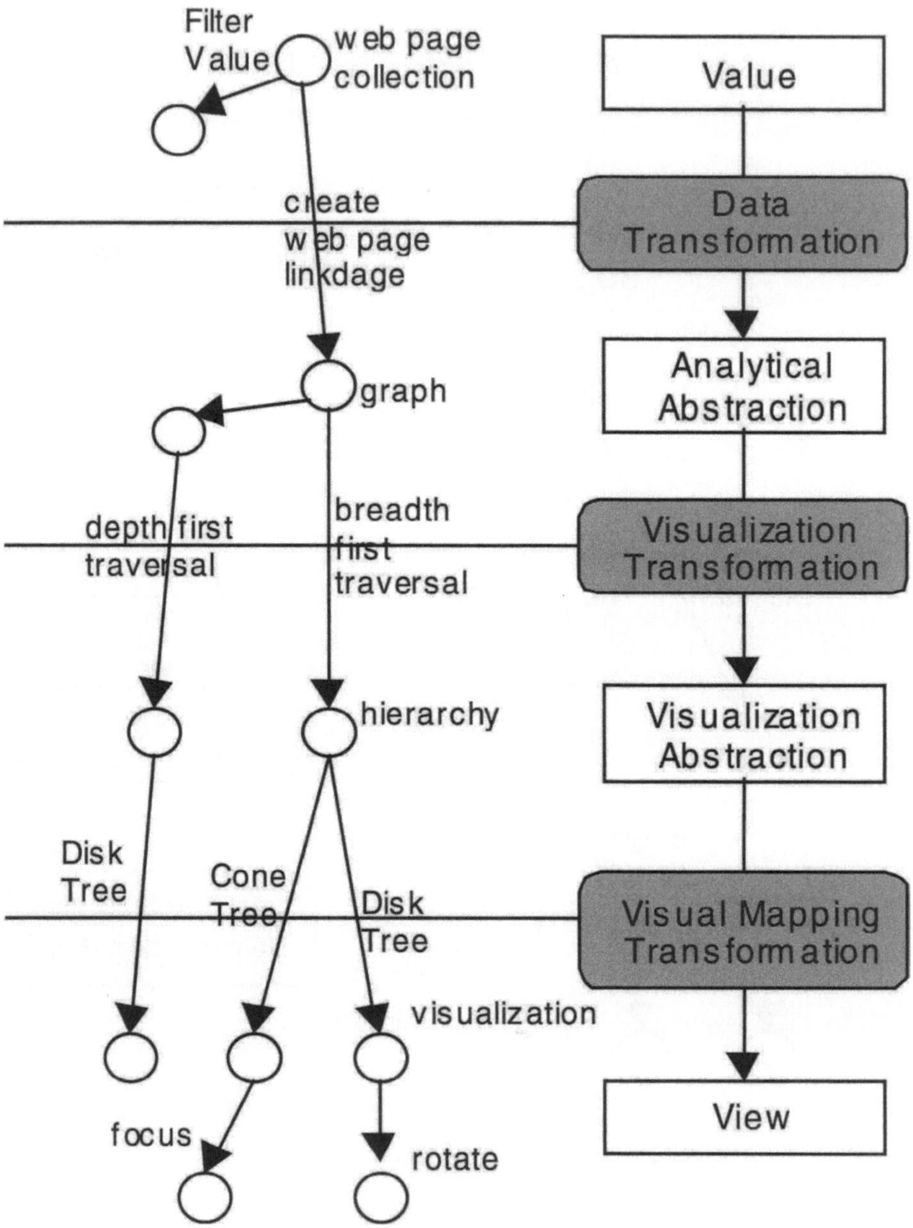

Figure 2.4. The Web Analysis Visualization Pipeline

Within View Stage Operators such as focusing and brushing nodes, or rotating the cone tree can then be applied to this visualized content.

We were interested in using visualization to perform Web site usage analysis. The case study is described in 6. Here we use this case study as an example of how we can apply the Data State Model to this analysis process. In this example, we used a large corporate Web site (Xerox.com), and here are the results:

- **Value**: For the exploration of Web ecologies, we chose the Xerox.com Web site over a one-year period from April 1997 to May 1998. The Xerox Web site contains roughly 7,500 HTML pages and 8,000 non-HTML items. The hyperlink topology and usage information were recorded on a daily basis.

- **Analytical Abstraction**:

  Content: The words in the page as well as clusters of items. For each page, we compute similarity to other pages using Spreading Activation [15]. Using this information, we can show relevance of other files to a given file.

  Usage: For each file, the frequency of page requests was aggregated using one-week intervals. The transition matrix, or hop count, from one node to another was also computed

  Topology: The hyperlink structure of the site was extracted from the HTML pages.

- **Visualization Abstraction**:

  Tree: The result of the Breadth First Traversal is a hierarchy of items with back links.

  Item Attribute: Each item stores its associated access frequency and hop counts[2]. Each item also contains information on its life cycle (newly created, deleted, moved, or modified).

  Item Vector: Each item also has a set of vectors that specify the precomputed Spreading Activation patterns. Moreover, the Spreading Activation is computed over the evolving document collection, which enables the comparison of results from different time periods.

4. Classification of Operators using the Framework

Using the above model, we can classify a variety of operators according to what stage of the pipeline the operator is involved in. The classification of visualization operators shows that each

[2]the number of times a particular link to its children is traveled

operator either performs a transformation that takes information between stages, or generates another information set within the same stage. That is, some operators work within a single stage, while other operators work across different stages. For example, a value-filtering operator selects a subset of the data and produces a new data set that does not have a new data format. Therefore, the value-filtering operator is a *Within Stage Operator*.

We have already described the *Between Stage Operators*, which were presented in Table 2.2: *Data Transformation Operators*, *Visualization Transformation Operators*, and *Visual Mapping Transformation Operators*.

There are four types of *Within Stage Operators*, and they correspond to the four stages of the information visualization pipeline. They are *Data Stage Operators*, *Analytical Abstraction Stage Operators*, *Visualization Abstraction Stage Operators*, and *View Stage Operators*.

Here we present some examples of each seven types of operators. The left hand side shows the domain that is associated with the example operators. The right hand side shows the various example operators that came from that data domain.

Data Stage Operators (DSO). .
General: value-filtering, subsetting
Domain Algebraic: difference or addition of two data sets
Image: flip, rotate, crop, Fourier transform, etc.
Point set: value-filter
Web: collection of Web pages generated by crawling a Web site

Data Transformation Operators (DTO). .
Textual: computing textual vectors, obtain ratings, create similarity relationships
Grid: iso-surface extraction
Point set: triangulation
Web: hypertext document network

Analytical Abstraction Stage Operators (AASO). .
Vector: select a subset of the vectors
Surface: divide region
Web: select subset of the the nodes in the network

Visualization Transformation Operators (VTO). .
Dimension Reduction: multi-dimensional scaling or principal

component analysis
Clustering: association rule, multi-modal clustering, spreading activation
Network: breadth first traversal, depth first traversal

Visualization Abstraction Stage Operators (VASO). .
Grid: simplify by reducing number of regions
Network: simplify by consolidating nodes
Hierarchy: cut-off depth of tree

Visual Mapping Transformation Operators (VMTO). .
Point set: scatter plot
Multi-dimensional Surfaces: World-within-World,
Hierarchy: Cone trees [87], Hyperbolic Trees [83], TreeMaps [56] and Disk Trees [28]
Network: GV3D [42], NVB [68], SeeNet [9]

View Stage Operators (VSO). .
Object Manipulation: rotation, translation, scale, zoom
Camera: position and orientation
General: view-filter

Spanning the pipeline.. For simple data domains where the visualization pipeline contains only two stages, we get only full view and value stage operators. For instance, for the domain of graphical images, there is a straight-forward mapping from the value (floating point values) to the view (pixels). Using only view/value stages becomes a succinct way of viewing the visualization pipeline.

In more complex data domains, there are operators throughout the entire pipeline. Often there will be several different choices that generate different analytical or visualization abstractions. For example, in textual analysis, there are several different kinds of textual analysis algorithms, such as clustering, multi-dimensional scaling, principal component analysis, collaborative filtering, etc. Each of these algorithms may require different analytical abstractions, such as textual vectors, similarity scoring, or user ratings.

4.1 Example: Web Analysis Visualization Operators

Here we will present a more extensive classification within a single complex data domain. In the next section, we will present a visualization spreadsheet example that analyzes Web usage data. At the heart of our Web Analysis Visualization Spreadsheet is the set of Web Analysis Visualization Operators (WAVO). Here we present the details of these operators in the context of the Data State Model in Table 2.3.

The data extraction based Data Transformation Operators near the top of Table 2.3 are hypertext specific, and require certain file formats for the extraction operators to work correctly. Since all Web sites are composed of HTML files, these operators are reusable across different Web sites, no matter how complex or large.

Some of the operators developed as part of this analysis suite can be used to analyze and visualize other hierarchical data sets. For example, Breadth First Traversal Visualization Transformation Operator and the hierarchical display techniques in the Visual Mapping Transformation Operator category.

The set of WAVO operators developed here is significant because it provides a framework for Web analysis visualizations. This framework allows users to understand the tools that are provided to them, and enable them to choose and execute these operators at their will. In other words, the formulation of these operators enables the on-the-fly analysis.

5. Properties of the Framework

Why is this framework powerful? The Data State Model provides a classification that is powerful because it makes several properties of operators explicitly clear. Earlier we described how an operator model needed to encompasses the view/value and operational similarity properties of operators. In addition to examining these two properties in detail, we also discuss how this Data State Model describes an operator-centric approach. We then discuss how the classification of operators using this Data State Model describes the the amount of direct manipulation that is possible in each operator, and the choices that we have in implementing these operators.

5.1 View versus Value

The closer an operator is to the view end of the pipeline, the more it takes on view operator properties. Similarly, the closer an operator is to the value end of the pipeline, the more it takes on value operator properties.

Type	operator	Description
Within Value	Filter-Value	Create a subset of the data. For example, create a subset of data containing only files that are reachable within four clicks of the root node.
Data Transformation	Extract linkage information	Create linkage graph from the hypertext files.
	Extract usage information	Produce daily summarization of each file's access frequency and the usage flow from one file to another (hop count).
Within Analytical Abstraction	Cluster nodes	Produce classes of the items, as well as identify groups of users, using several different clustering algorithms.
Visualization Transformation	Breadth First Traversal	Generate a hierarchy that can be visualized using various tree visualization techniques. Since the Xerox web site is highly hierarchical in nature, this generates a useful view of the entire site.
Within Visualization Abstraction	Usage Frequency Pattern Algebra	Generates a frequency pattern over the web site, which can then be subtracted/added/averaged with other patterns from other weeks.
	Spreading Activation Pattern Algebra	Compare/aggregate Spreading Activation patterns by subtracting/ adding one with another.
Visual Mapping Transformation	Display Disk Tree	Layout hierarchy based on a planar circle. This is our primary visualization technique used to visualize large hierarchies. Because it is a 2D technique, we can embed additional attributes using glyphs on the third dimension.
	Display Cone Tree	Layout hierarchy based on a 3D cone. A 3D hierarchy visualization technique that shows the various levels in the tree extremely well.
	Apply Coloring Pattern	Map color onto a displayed tree based on numeric item attributes.
	Display Pattern Glyph	Show the Spreading Activation pattern on top of the Disk Tree using glyphs. Each pattern consists of pairs of <item, activation strength>.
Within View	Geometric Operators	Rotate, translate, zoom, scale, etc.
	Detail-on-demand Zoom	Fly directly to the selected item for close examination.
	Animation	Show several disk trees in succession.

Table 2.3. The Web Analysis Visualization Operators

Figure 2.5 illustrates the addition operator at different levels of the Data State Model. Figure 2.5(a) shows an visualization addition operator that operates at the view level, where the pixel values are determined. The system takes two data sets, and generates two visualization representations, which in turn determines the two views as bitmaps. These two bitmaps are then added pixel by pixel to generate a new bitmap. This is an example of a within view stage operator.

Figure 2.5(b) shows an example of a within visualization representation operator, which takes two polygon visualization representations and adds the two polygon lists together to form a new polygon visualization representation, which in turn is rendered into a bitmap view. The example shows that because the operator processes the information at the polygon level, the user can rotate the geometric content.

Figure 2.5(c) shows an example of a within data stage operator, which takes two raw data sets and adds them together to form a new data set. The data set is then processed into a new set of polygons, and a new bitmap view is generated. The example shows that because the underlying data set is changed dramatically, the visualization algorithm may produce a view that is significantly different from the views generated from the two original raw data sets.

The Data State Model makes these differences explicitly clear, thus making end-users, designers, and implementors aware of these issues. Upon realizing these choices, implementors must examine the application requirements to decide which of these different operators should be implemented. Because of this framework, we can even ensure application-independent operators, such as the pixel-oriented operators we described above, are implemented within the architecture of our software system, making re-implementation unnecessary.

5.2 Applicability of Operators

The breadth of applicability of an operator is dependent on how similar it is operationally to other operators in the system. Earlier we described the issue of operational similarity for operators. Between two operators, the more operationally similar they are to each other, the more actual code they can share. Code sharing means that it is possible to create templates for these operators, thus reducing the amount of re-implementation.

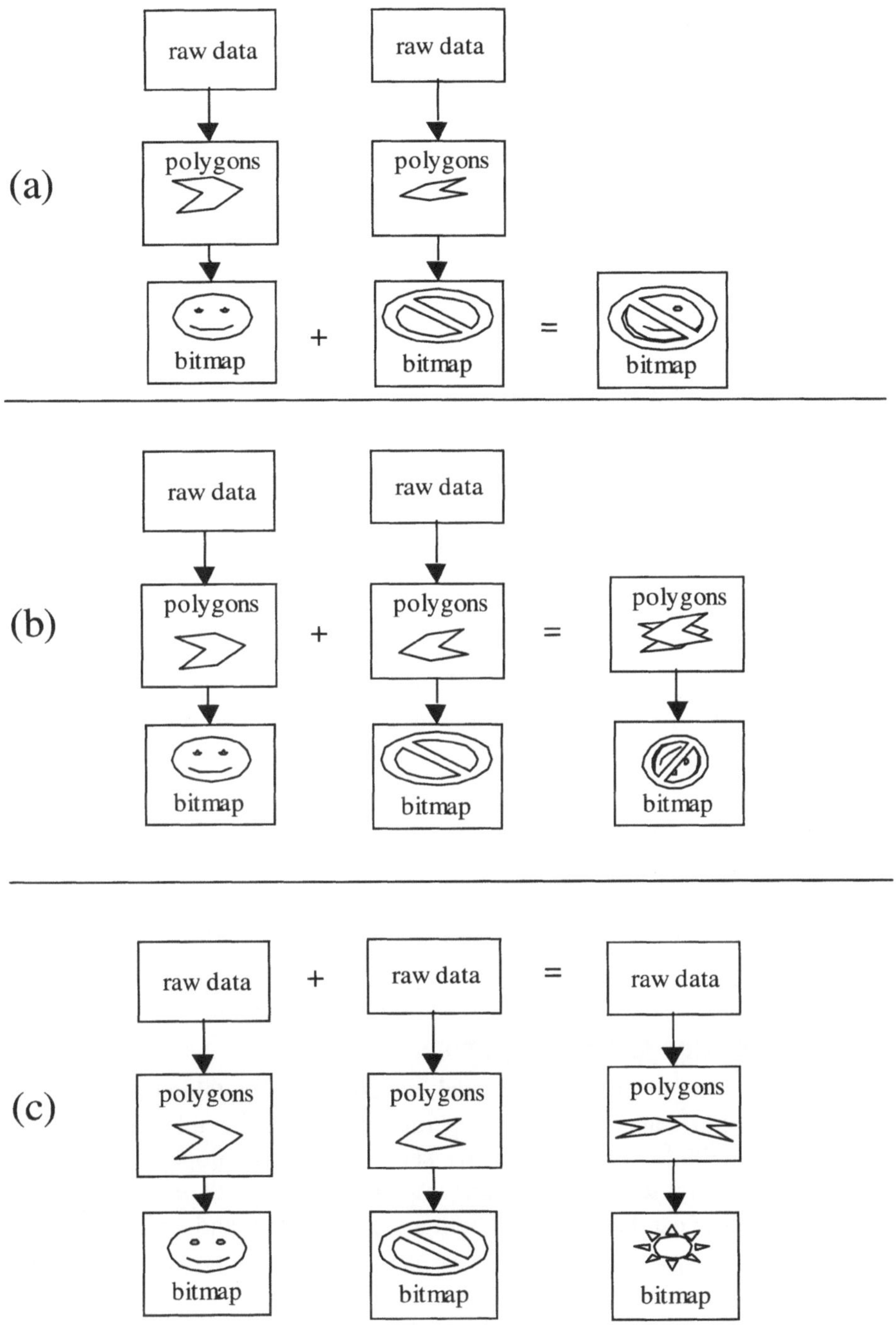

Figure 2.5. Multiple level of semantics for the addition operator at different stages of the visualization pipeline.

The Data State Model helps in describing this phenomenon. The breadth of an operator is dependent on how late it comes in the visualization pipeline. Moving down the pipeline gets us closer and closer to a generalized data type that is applicable over a wider range of data domains. For example, rotation, scaling, and other scene operators tend to have very broad applicability, because view operators mostly operate on geometric primitives.

In order of decreasing breadth of applicability, we list some examples of the following different levels of applicability:

- As mentioned in Section 3, *View Stage Operator*s, such as rotation, are applicable across a large set of data domains, because they operate on computer graphic geometric primitives such as lines and polygons.
- *Visual Mapping Transformation Operator*s are usually applicable to a wide variety of data types. For example, glyphs, icons, streamlines can be employed to show multi-dimensional data at a particular spatial point. Worlds-within-Worlds [37] can be used to visualize high dimensional surfaces. Cone Trees [87], Hyperbolic Trees [59], TreeMaps [56] and Disk Trees [28] can be used to visualize a wide variety of hierarchical data.
- *Visualization Transformation Operator*s can be applied to data domains with similar goals. For example, multi-dimensional clustering can be used to reduce the dimensionality of any problem that can be formulated using a feature space. Breadth-first traversal can be used to produce a hierarchy out of a graph network.
- *Data Transformation operator*s are specific to the particular data structure from an application domain, because they take the data structure as input, and output an analytical abstraction. Examples include creating text vectors from a list of documents, or creating a graph network from a web site.
- *Value Stage Operator*s are specific to its associated data type.

5.3 Operator-Centric Approach

In our Data State Model, we are explicitly taking an operator-centric approach. If an operator appears to be able to operate on multiple types of data, we separate the single operator idea into several different operator implementations. As an example, if a filter can be viewed as both a value operator and a view operator, we separate these two meanings into a value-filter and a view-filter operator.

This approach is the opposite of the data-centric approach, which favors overloading operators so that they can function with multiple data types. The data-centric approach has the advantage of simplifying the space of different operators. This presents a simpler end-user model at the cost of complexity on the part of the designer. The data-centric approach also sometimes creates semantic ambiguities that are very confusing to the end-user, as we saw in the HomeFinder view/value-filtering example at the beginning of the chapter. Moreover, the added simplification of the operator space in the data-centric approach does not represent significant complexity savings. Since a visualization system needs to deal with many different data types, the operator space of such systems will be very complex anyway.

Our operator-centric approach is a significant departure from past visualization models, and gives the Data State Model the ability to classify different operators in finer grain detail. By taking the approach of classifying the space of operators in finer detail, we can more easily reuse operator definitions, and actual code implementations. This in turn will be a benefit to the end-user, because there is little ambiguity in the semantics of the operator, as each operator is precisely defined in its inputs and outputs.

5.4 Direct Manipulation

The amount of direct manipulation that is possible in an operator also lies on the visualization pipeline scale. The closer the operator is to view, the higher the amount of interactivity is possible, because the operation has a visualization to manipulate. For example, the geometric position and orientation operators are easily directly manipulated. As described in Section 5.3, variable-to-axis mapping in our SSR system is a Visualization Transformation Operator that can easily be specified using a point-and-click approach with dialogs and menus.

As we move up the pipeline toward value operators, the amount of domain-dependency increases, making the specification of these operations more and more difficult, because near the raw value end of the pipeline, operators do not directly perform on a visualization. For example, the parsing of a file for data extraction is a Data Transformation Operator, and it is extremely hard to design an interface that allows the user to specify the file format. Interestingly, MS Excel has certain amount of automatic parsing capabilities using an 'Import Wizard'. This is because the need to import data is especially important to its users. Such capabilities are hard to design for information visualization, because the wide variety of data domains has different data and information structures. Indeed, for many visualization systems, the hardest part of the visualization process is importing the data,

5.5 Implementation Choices

A model should also help us choose implementation methods for the operators. What does the classification of the operators tell us about how they can be implemented? More specifically, if multiple pieces of software modules are used in putting together a visualization application, where should a particular operator be implemented? There are three basic choices for implementation:

- Inside the visualization system. Examples of operators appropriate for this choice are scene operators, camera operators, color scale operators.

- Using queries inside a data management engine, such as a database management system (DBMS). For example, we can use the full power of relational algebra to organize and use OnLine Analytical Processing (OLAP) to analyze and generate the meta-data.

- Using an analytical engine outside of both the data depository and the visualization system. Examples are differential equation solvers for fluid-flow simulations, Web crawlers, numerical analysis in Mathematica, Maple, Matlab, business computation using numeric spreadsheet in MS Excel, or image, sound, video processing in Khoros.

The Data State operator model also helps us in choosing between these implementation choices. For example, if an operator is closer to the view stage in the pipeline, then it is most efficient and most easily implemented in the visualization system. Data flow systems such as AVS [8] and Data Explorer [50], and our Visualization Spreadsheet [30] implement most, if not all, of its visual mapping transformation operators and view operators in the visualization system.

Often the data source of a visualization comes from a data analytical engine such as a relational database. In these cases, if an operator is closer to the value stage of the pipeline, then it is often more efficient to implement it in the database management system. For example, a merge data set operation is often a simple 'join' command in a relational database.

6. Discussion

6.1 Three Classes of Users of this Model

Three kinds of people can benefit from this framework. First, this framework provides a clean and concise model for end-users to understand how to operate a general visualization system and to predict the results of applying operators. The usability of the system is enhanced by bridging the gulf of execution because users can more predictablly understand how operators are suppose to affect values and views in the system. In our experience, this kind of predictability is crucial in the success of the Visualization Spreadsheet.

Second, application programmers can use this model to extend general visualization system to new data domains. This framework enables programmers to identify operators that are not domain-specific and, hence, that they can easily reuse. For example, in the Visualization Spreadsheet, the system must be extended with domain-specific analysis operators such as textual document clustering and visualization to enable it to be applicable in specific application tasks, such as analyzing financial documents. In order for application programmers to profitably extend a general visualization system, there must be a consistent operator framework that help them structure or reuse visualization components.

Lastly, visualization system developers can use this framework to make the system extensible to the application programmer. The Data State Model forces developers to think clearly about operators and how they relate to the view/value spectrum. Builders of general visualization systems are thus encouraged to have modular and extensible systems for specific application domains. For example, in our experience, we have applied this framework to our Visualization Spreadsheet system and extended it to multiple data domains, which we present in Chapter 5.

6.2 End-User Advantages using this Framework

Of these three types of users, the end-user matters most, because the visualization model must help the end-users achieve their goals faster and easier. For example, how does the Data State Model help the end-user when using the visualization spreadsheet? Empirically, we have some end-user experiences with this framework in our Visualization Spreadsheet system. In our experience, the development of this framework enhances the usability of the spreadsheet by solving the following three problems.

First, the framework provides an user interaction model so that users can understand what they have to do to get a visualization. This is accomplished by incorporating the visualization pipeline process model. By following the steps in the pipeline, the user can perform the actions required to create a desired visualization in the correct order.

Second, the framework establishes users' expectation of the flow of changes to the data. This enables users to understand how the system works, and how the data flow can be manipulated to perform the correct analysis action. For example, let us create a set of textual feature vectors from a set of documents (see the left side of Figure 2.2). In one analysis, we choose to do multidimensional scaling, and in another analysis we choose to first create a subset of these textual vectors before applying a clustering algorithm. Because both states are dependent on the same data source, if the set of documents change, both states would change as well. This is made explicit by the Data State Model.

Third, the framework cleanly solves the operator semantics problem, because it models the separation between view and value. The view versus value filtering example mentioned in the introduction of this chapter is an excellent example of how the framework forces interaction designers to realize potential ambiguity in the semantics of operators. By forcing designers to think about where operators exist in the pipeline, the operator semantics are made explicit. By having a cleaner model, the end-user can now choose among several operational semantics that correspond to the correct action that she desires. The user can interact more accurately because she understands how operators in different stages of the pipeline fit together.

7. Summary

In the past several years, researchers have made great advances in information visualization. Semiologies of graphic representation methods have been developed by various researchers [14, 65, 24] to gain understanding of the visualization design space. In this chapter, we extended this research to include a framework for visualization interactions and operators. We contributed to a new way of thinking about the operator model that applies over a range of data domains, with some specific discussion as applied to visualization spreadsheets:

1 Establishing a new operator-centric framework for designers to explore the following properties of operators in visualization systems: view vs. value, domain dependence/independence, breadth of applicability, amount of direct manipulation possible, and implementation choices.

2 Developing a new end-user interaction model that establishes user expectation, thus enabling users to apply and predict the result of operators and the relationships they establish between views and values. We form an analysis process model for users to apply to their task scenario in their particular data domain.

3 Focusing on end-users' need for viewing intermediate results in determining subsequent analysis steps. We use a visualization Data State Model with multiple data values and views to bridge the "gulf of execution".

We examined recent work on visualization interaction frameworks and then developed a novel operator and user interaction model. Our Data State Model unifies the data analysis process and the complex relationship between view and value to characterize the interactive and non-interactive operations in a visualization system. For example, using the Data State Model as a basis, we developed a way to classify operators. We examined not just view and value, but how intermediate data and visualization abstractions are generated in the analysis process. We discuss the properties of this framework. For example, we suggested three possible ways of implementing operators based on where they are involved in the visualization pipeline.

The framework facilitates a new way of exploring the space of visualization operators. Using the Data State Model, this method forms the basis of an evaluation technique for operators in visualizations. By applying this operator analysis to various visualizations, we can point researchers toward areas where particular operators are missing from a given system or technique. We can also use this model to compare different interaction models in visualizations. This will enable other researchers to characterize various interaction techniques, and capture design requirements for new application domains, and develop new and novel operators.

Chapter 3

VALIDATION OF MODEL

What is "scientific research"? This is research which reduces the a priori *by justifying the answers....*

—Jacques Bertin [15, p. 265]

In this chapter, we validate the generality of the Data State Model visualization framework by showing that it can be applied to a wide range of visualization techniques. We describe the operators in each technique in the context of the Data State Model by using example data domains. In doing this, we illustrate the power of the Data State Model by showing its general comprehensive applicability.

We chose the various visualization techniques based on their familiarity to the information visualization community and their relevance to information visualization systems. This set of techniques spans a large area of the information visualization design space, as it is based on a previous taxonomy of information visualization design space [24]. We included all of the categories in [24], and further establish other examples. In looking at each of the visualization techniques, we first determine the raw data, and how it is obtained in the system. We then construct the visualization pipeline according to the description of each of the techniques in the literature.

This analysis shows how each of these visualization techniques would be implemented in the Data State Model and how it might be used in a visualization spreadsheet. For each of the visualization techniques, the result of this analysis helps us classify and choose how to implement the different operators, because the analysis implicitly specifies the dependencies that are induced between the operators.

For example, in the hierarchical techniques category, we included several major visualization techniques for viewing trees (Cone Tree [87], Disk Tree [28], Hyperbolic Browser [59], and TreeMap [56]). The techniques share similar data domains and operators in their visualization pipelines, except that each technique is a different Visual Mapping Transformation Operator that can operate on the same Visualization Abstractions. The operators' inputs and outputs then specifies the dependencies between the data. Regardless of which technique we have chosen to visualize the tree, we can then use these visualization operators to operate on hierarchical data.

In a visualization system that implements all of these operators, such as our Visualization Spreadsheet, we can explore the use of each of these four different representation techniques as we wish, since the operators in the visualization pipeline have been carefully categorized. The Data State Model helps in this categorization, which exposes the similarities and differences between each of the tree visualization techniques.

Visualization Technique	Within Value	Data Transformation	Within Analytical Abstraction	Visualization Transformation	Within Visualization Abstraction	Visual Mapping Transformation	Within View
Scientific Visualization							
Ozone Layer Visualization Treinish94	*Data: Ozone layer geographical information over time*	Extract geographical information samples into quantitative variables	Normalize samples and quantitative values	Direct spatial mapping of quantitative values to longitude, latitude, and height onto Earth		Map quantitative variables to longitude, latitude, and height; Map ozone level to color	Rotate, Scale, Animate; Change colormap
Geographical-based Visualization							
Profit Landscape Visible Decisions	*Data: Profit statistics linked to geographical regions*	Extract into quantitative variables	Normalize sample	Direct spatial mapping of geo-coordinate variables		Map geo-coordinate variables onto a geographical map; Map profit variable to glyph (size of lines)	Rotate, Scale, Animate; Change colormap
Multi-dimensional Plots							
Dynamic Querying Ahlberg94	*Example data: Home, Movies sales data*	Parse into feature records		Create multi-dimensional point sets	Dynamic value-filtering; Apply unmapped variable filtering	Map into scatter plot; Choosing variables-to-axes mappings	Dynamic view-filtering
Parallel Coordinates Inselberg97	*Example data sets: production run of VLSI chip yield and its defect parameters*	Extract corresponding yield and parameter feature set	Choosing a subset of records using dynamic value-filtering	Create point set from records	*Visualization Abstraction: Point set*	Plot point set using parallel coordinates	Dynamic view-filtering; Sorting of axis; Interactive permutation of axis
World-Within-World Feiner 93	*Data: High-dimensional point set or surfaces* Dynamic value-filtering		Normalize samples			Map high dimensional surface to local area	Dynamic view-filtering; Rotate, Scale, Focus

Table 3.1. Various visualization techniques analyzed using the Data State Model

Visualization Technique	Within Value	Data Transformation	Within Analytical Abstraction	Visualization Transformation	Within Visualization Abstraction	Visual Mapping Transformation	Within View
Multi-dimensional Tables							
Table Lens Rao94a,Rao95	*Data: baseball player statistics*	Parse statistics into numeric records	*Analytical Abstraction: Numeric records* Sort records	Construct numeric table from records	*Visualization Abstraction: Constructed numeric table*	Represent number using bars, with focus+context distortion-based table	Change distortion focus
Information Landscapes and Spaces							
Perspective Wall Mackinlay91	*Example Data: Schedule, File system*	Parse information into records	*Analytical Abstraction: Parsed record set* Dynamic value-filtering of records	Create linear list of records	*Visualization Abstraction: Linear list with item features*	Create wall panels in 3D with glyphs, with focus+context distortion-based display	Focus on a particular wall; Focus an item; Dynamic view-filter; Choose different levels of detail
Trees							
Hierarchical Techniques: Cone tree (Robertson91), Hyperbolic Browser (Lamping95), TreeMap (Johnson91), DiskTree (Chi98)	*Data: File system; Organization charts; Hypertext or Web linkage structure*	Extract into graph	*Analytical Abstraction: Graph* Apply dynamic value-filtering of nodes or edges	Do breadth first traversal	*Visualization Abstraction: Tree hierarchy*	Layout using 3D cones; Layout using hyperbolic tree; Layout using Disk Tree; Layout using space filling approaches such as TreeMap	Focus node; Hide subtree; Change orientation and position of tree; Apply Dynamic level-filtering

Table 3.2. Various visualization techniques analyzed (continued)

Visualization Technique	Within Value	Data Transformation	Within Analytical Abstraction	Visualization Transformation	Within Visualization Abstraction	Visual Mapping Transformation	Within View
Node and Link							
SeeNet Becker95 Comment: added view/value filtering semantics, aggregation is mentioned as implemented using data management software, several different views of the data sets.	*Example data sets: phone calls made; Internet packet flows; Email communication patterns*		*Analytical abstraction: parsed records of source and destination and associated feature sets* Unmapped variable value-filtering; Choose variables of displayed statistics; Aggregate records		*Visualization Abstraction: Graphs, and Networks*	Display graph as matrix, geographical linkmaps, or nodemaps	For all three views: Sound feedback; Unmapped variable view-filtering (they called it 'conditioning')
							For matrix display: Threshold time view-slider; Permute rows and columns
							For nodemaps and linkmaps: Change Size, Color, Zoom; Parameter focusing; Identification by brushing; Change animation speed; Change line thickness, or line length; Dynamic query threshold view-slider
							For nodemaps: Change symbol size; Use color sensitivity view-slider

Table 3.3. Various visualization techniques analyzed (continued)

Visualization Technique	Within Value	Data Transformation	Within Analytical Abstraction	Visualization Transformation	Within Visualization Abstraction	Visual Mapping Transformation	Within View
Text							
AlignmentViewer Chi96	*Data: Similarity reports from comparing a single sequence against a database of many other sequences*	Parsing textual reports; Addition, Subtraction between different reports; Unmapped variable value-filtering	*Analytical Abstraction: Alignment records (data structure representing parsed information)*	Extracting information from records	*Visualization Abstraction: Feature point set with vector*	Map into comb-glyphs	Rotation, Translate Zoom; Focus on a single alignment; Detail-on-demand; Animation (by using an iterator over the view-filtering)
ThemeScape and Galaxies Wise95	*Data: CNN news stories*	Create textual word frequency vector; Choose an item and then perform weighted query	*Analytical Abstraction: Text vectors*	Multi-dimensional scaling; Principal component analysis		Map into surfaces of hills and valleys	Zoom, Rotate; Focus on detail spot For ThemeScape: Create slices For Galaxies: Animate scatter plot
WebBook and WebForager Card96	*Data: URLs for web pages*	Retrieve web pages; Generate images of each Web page	*Analytical Abstraction: Images of HTML pages generated by getting the Web pages*	Create linear list of pages; Aggregate into a book or a pile; Place pile on book shelf (creating list of lists); Crawl from a URL and create a book from the collection	*Visualization Abstraction: Linear page lists, Collection of page lists.* Merge page lists; Merge collections of page lists	Create books with multiple pages; View using Document Lens; Create bookshelf, table, piles	Focus on a book; Focus on a page; Flip through pages in a book; View book using Document Lens; Put onto history pile

Table 3.4. Various visualization techniques analyzed (continued)

Visualization Technique	Within Value	Data Transformation	Within Analytical Abstraction	Visualization Transformation	Within Visualization Abstraction	Visual Mapping Transformation	Within View
Web Visualization							
Time Tube Chi98	*Data: web structure evolving over time and its associated usage statistics (Content, Usage, and Topology of the web site)*	Create graph from web structure by crawling the web site	*Analytical Abstraction: Evolving graph represented as ordered collection of graph*	Do breadth first traversal with global node position over time	*Visualization Abstraction: Evolving tree as ordered list of trees*	Create Time Tube, which is represented using an aggregation of Disk Trees (invisible tube--like shelf)	Recognize gestures for: Focus on a slice; Bring slices back into the Time Tube; Zooming focus on the connectivity of a node by right-clicking on it; Rotate slices; Brushing on pages by highlight URL on all slices; Animate through the slices
Spreadsheets							
Spreadsheet for Images Levoy94	*Data, Analytical and Visualization Abstraction: pixels, voxels* Rotate Image; Filter; Change color scale; and other image processing mechanisms						*View: images from pixels, volumes from voxels (direct mapping from data to view)* Rotate image; Filter; Change color scale; and other image processing operations; Rocking the volume visualization

Table 3.5. Various visualization techniques analyzed (continued)

Visualization Technique	Within Value	Data Transformation	Within Analytical Abstraction	Visualization Transformation	Within Visualization Abstraction	Visual Mapping Transformation	Within View
FINESSE Varshney96	*Data: Financial data*	Compute call and put option prices	*Analytical Abstraction: Matrix records, Mathematical functions* Change parameter of functions; Change arithmetic relationships	Compute curves from math function models	*Visualization Abstraction: Matrix, Computed curves*	Create heat map; Create surfaces in 3D; Plot using 3D bar charts; 2D line plots; Create text for filenames; Represent variables using value sliders	Change orientation of geometric objects; Change to common colormap or font; View using same geometric orientation; Show cell dependency relationships; Picking a data item, Input math function
Spreadsheet for Information Visualization Chi97infovis Comment: allows value and view Dependencies between cells	*Example data sets: Point sets; Matrix; Sequence similarity reports; Web structure, Web usage pattern; etc.*	Normalize matrices; Parse textual reports; Create random point sets; Create graph from web structure by crawling the web site	*Analytical Abstraction: Normalized matrix and point sets; Value tuples; Evolving graph represented as ordered collection of graph* Dynamic value-filter; Algebraic data set operators	Perform Delaunay Triangulation; Extract data features from records; Do breadth first traversal with global node position over time	*Visualization Abstraction: Point set; Matrix; Triangulated surface; Point set with feature vector; hierarchy, list of trees; etc.*	Create heat map, matrix cube visualization, matrix bar visualization, Cone Tree, Disk Tree, glyphs, scatter plot; Choosing variable-to-axes mapping; Change cells to share same visual mapping Transformation	Dynamic view-filter; Change object position and orientation; Pixel image addition between cells; Geometric object addition between cells; Animation; Coordinated direct manipulation
Web Analysis using Visualization Spreadsheet Chi 98	*Date: Web site usage analysis* Filter-Value	Extract linkage information; Extract usage information	Cluster nodes	Breadth First Traversal	Perform usage frequency pattern algebra; Apply Spreading Activation pattern algebra	Display Disk Tree; Display Cone Tree; Apply Coloring Pattern; Display Pattern Glyph	Apply geometric operators; Detail-on-demand Zoom; Animation

Table 3.6. Various visualization techniques analyzed (continued)

Chapter 4

EXPRESSIVENESS OF DATA STATE MODEL

Graphics is a very simple language. Its laws become self-evident when we recognize that the image is transformable, that it must be reordered, and that its transformations represent a visual form of information-processing.

—Jacques Bertin [15, p. 183]

Visualization transforms data into graphical forms to be represented on the computer display. Hence, visualization deals with both *transformations* and *representations*. Transformation is the process that converts data into graphical primitives. Representation is the data structures that are used to handle and store the various outputs of these processes.

Traditional visualization data flow networks [98, 103, 43, 54, 8, 50] have concentrated on the various transformations that are necessary to generate a computer display. These data flow networks are typically depicted graphically by drawing a network with nodes representing data transformation processes, and directional edges representing how data flows from one process to another. Experience in the visualization field has shown that the Data Flow Model is an effective visual programming model that lets users build an application by integrating modular components.

We introduced the Data State Model in Chapter 2. At first glance it has very similar characteristics to the Data Flow Model. For instance, both models use nodes and edges to transcribe the visualization process. Both models use these graphs to describe how data sets travel through the processing mechanism. However, there is an important difference. Data State Model captures distinct data states, whereas the Data Flow Model captures the order of distinct processes that comprise of a visualization. This difference is reflected in that the Data Flow Model uses nodes to denote processes and edges to denote data flow directions, whereas the Data State Model uses nodes to denote data states and edges to denote processes.

Given these differences, our research question here is two-fold. On the one hand, we are interested in understanding the following question: "What is the relationship between the functionality of the Data State Model and the Data Flow Model?" Is one model more expressive than the other? If we are given an Data Flow Model, can we build a Data State Model that produces the same output? For example, are there certain visualization constructions that are not possible with the Data State Model? User experiences and commercial success have established the capability of data flow visualization systems and the expressiveness of the Data Flow Model. By comparing the Data State Model with it, we can learn the merits of each model. Here we show that the Data State Model is as expressive as the Data Flow model, and vice versa. We present a duality transformation between the two models. Using the duality transformation, we show that the two models are equally expressive.

On the other hand, expressiveness is only part of the picture. The difference in the emphasis of each model creates user interfaces that result in differences in the user experience. So the second question we are interested in gaining some understanding is "what are the advantages and disadvantages of the two models?" What makes one model more appropriate in a situation than the other model? We discuss the advantages and disadvantages of the two models for a variety of user tasks.

1. Expanding the Data Flow Model

To construct a flow chart is to process information.
—Jacques Bertin [15, p. 136]

States vs. Stages. The Data Flow Model uses nodes to represent processes because the model focuses on the data transformations. The edges represent the flow of the data from one process stage to the next. A edge exists only if a process transforms the data into a new form. Often, in data flow networks, the data state is not explicitly represented by distinct edges. In other words, the edges represent data *stages* instead of *states*. For example, consider a single data flow chart that constructs a scatter plot (raw data set → extract point set → create scatter plot → view). Consider applying two different data sets to this flow chart. Since the model does not capture data states, these two different data set can flow down the same pipes, even though a different data set clearly represents a different data state. In the Data Flow Model, since the format of the data does not change, there is neither new edges nor new nodes to represent this.

In order for the Data Flow Model to capture the same amount of detail as the Data State Model, we first define a canonical form of the Data Flow Model that insists on having each edge representing only a single distinct data state. The implication of this is that we force the Data Flow Model to capture more details of the visualization process. The syntax and semantics of the model remain the same. However, this change does not fundamentally change the Data Flow Model, as it still shows how data flows through the system and how processes and algorithms transform the data. The model still shows the functional dependencies between the processes. This definition simply expands the Data Flow Model based on data set instances.

Definition 4.1 *The* **canonical form** *of the Data Flow Model restricts each edge to represent only a single data state.*

Below, we will show that the canonical form of the Data Flow Model is just as expressive as the Data State Model. By expanding the notion of data flow network in this way, we can then show the equivalence of the Data Flow Model and the Data State Model.

2. Visualization Equivalence

In this section, we first introduce the notion of equivalence between two visualization models by defining the idea of expressiveness of the visualization model. Then we use a duality transformation to show that one model can be transformed into the other and generate the correct output.

We first ask the question, "what is a visualization model?" A visualization model describes a visualization process, which is a transformation process. A transformation process is composed of a series of transformation steps. So we first define the visualization transformation. We will use a mathematical functional description:

Definition 4.2 *A* ***visualization transformation*** *or* ***visualization operator*** n *processes information d from a domain D and maps it into information d in a different domain D'.* $n(d) = d'$, *where* $d \in D$ *and* $d' \in D'$.

The domain specifies the structure of the information. A domain may be as simple as the set of natural numbers, or as complex as database records of user transactions with a hypertext system. For example, a genetic sequence similarity alignment record computed using the BLAST program is a single element in the genetic sequence similarity domain. A domain may be a visualization domain, which means that the elements in that domain are mapped or easily mapable onto the display screen. A domain may be a data domain, which means the elements in that domain are raw data that are not yet mapped onto the display screen.

Definition 4.3 *A* **visualization function** m *is a visualization transformation that maps from a data domain D to a visualization domain* V. *So given* $d \in D$, $m(d) = v$, *where* $v \in V$. *Typically,* m *is composed of a series of visualization transformations from a set of transformations* $N = n_1, n_2, \ldots$. *Each transformation* n_i *in a series maps from a domain* D_i *to* D'_i. *The domain of the next transformation in the series must be the same as* D'_i. *For example, if* $m_3 = (n_2, n_3, n_2, n_1)$, *then applying* m_3 *to d gives* $m_3(d) = n_1(n_2(n_3(n_2(d))))$, *where* $d \in D_2$, $n_2(d) \in D'_2 = D_3$, $n_3(n_2(d)) \in D'_3 = D_2$, *and so on.*

The output of a visualization transformation may not be compatible with the input of another visualization transformation. This is because each visualization transformation takes a specific kind of data from a domain as input. Therefore, not all visualization transformations can be composed together, and we cannot simply construct a composition of an arbitrary series of visualization transformations. The input domain of a transformation must be the same as the output domain of another transformation for the two transformations to be connected in a series.

Definition 4.4 *A* ***visualization model*** M *is a set of visualization functions* $M = m_1, m_2, m_3, \ldots$.

An **instance** of a visualization model is a particular application, case, or example of the visualization model. The act of constructing a case is called **instantiation**.

Definition 4.5 *In the Definition above, each* m_i *is an* **instance** *of* M, *and* $m_i(d)$ *is an* **instantiation** *of* M.

A model is a series of transformations, which can be viewed as a mapping function from data to view. An instance is a particular defined series of transformation designed for a particular type of data.

Next, we define the relation "as-expressive-as":

Definition 4.6 *We say a visualization model A is* ***as-expressive-as*** *another model B if given an instance b of B, we can find a model a of A such that for all inputs i, $a(i)$ gives exactly the same output as $b(i)$. (That is, given $b \in B$ and for all inputs i, $\exists a \in A$ such that $a(i) = b(i)$.)*

Notice that expressiveness is not a symmetric relation (A being as-expressive-as B does not mean B is as-expressive-as A). However, it does define a pre-order relation because it is reflexive (A is as-expressive-as A) and transitive (A is as-expressive-as B and B is as-expressive-as C implies that A is as-expressive-as C). To prove transitivity, we know given $b \in B$ and some input i, $\exists a \in A$ such that $a(i) = b(i)$. We also know that given $c \in C$ and same input i, $\exists b \in B$ such that $b(i) = c(i)$. This means that given $c \in C$ and input i, we can instantiate $b \in B$ and $a \in A$, such that $a(i) = b(i) = c(i)$. Therefore, A is as-expressive-as C.

Next, we use the concept of antisymmetric relation to define the meaning of equivalence between two visualization models. A relation R is antisymmetric if for all x and y, xRy and yRx implies $x == y$.

Definition 4.7 *We say that two visualization models are* **equivalent in visualization expressiveness** *if and only if A is* as-expressive-as *B and B is* as-expressive-as *A.*

So the "as-expressive-as" relation is an antisymmetric relation. Since it is also reflexive and transitive, "as-expressive-as" is a partial ordering.

Given this Definition, we wish to show:

Theorem 4.1 *The Data State Model is equivalent in visualization expressiveness to the Data Flow Model.*

Proof: We will prove this by construction. Using a principle we call *Duality*, we will show that given an instance of the Data Flow Model we can construct a Data State Model that gives exactly the same output and vice versa. To prove this in both directions, we use the directed graph expression of both models and the duality transformation.

Using Data Flow Model notations, an instance m_i can be expressed as a path $p = n_i \xrightarrow{d_i} n_j \xrightarrow{d_j} n_k \xrightarrow{d_k} \ldots$ through a directed graph where the nodes are the transformation steps $N = n_i, n_j, n_k, \ldots$ and the data states $d_i, d_j, d_k, \ldots$ are the edges. Using the Data State Model notation, the same instance can be expressed as $p = d_i \xrightarrow{n_i} d_j \xrightarrow{n_j} d_k \xrightarrow{n_k} \ldots$, where the the nodes are the data states $d_i, d_j, d_k, \ldots$ and the edges are the transformation steps $N = n_i, n_j, n_k, \ldots$.

Duality Transformation. To perform the duality transformation [1], simply take each edge in the model and convert it into a node and convert each node into edges. Mathematically, given a model $G = (V, E)$, the duality transformation constructs $D(G) = G' = (V', E')$ where:

- For each edge e in $E(G)$, we construct a vertex v'_e in V', and
- For each node v in $V(G)$, for each pair of edges (e_1, e_2), where e_1 goes into v, and e_2 exits v, we construct an edge e' from v'_{e_1} to v'_{e_2}, where v'_{e_1} and v'_{e_2} are the corresponding vertices of e_1 and e_2 respectively in G'.

Note that in this transformation, a single node may have several corresponding dual edges. Figure 4.1 shows an example of this transformation.

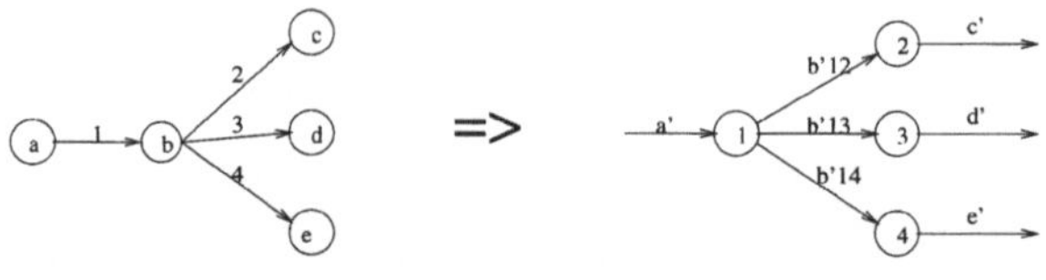

Figure 4.1. An example of the Duality Transformation

The duality transformation switches the role of the nodes and edges. For example, in one direction of this application, our state model $G = (V, E)$ uses nodes to represent data states, and edges to represent distinct processes. (V = *set of data states*, E = *set of transformation processes*). After the duality transformation, we obtain a $D(G)$ that has V' = *set of transformation processes* and E' = *set of data states*.

[1] This is not the same as the *dual graph* in graph theory. The dual graph $dual(G)$ of a graph G constructs a node for each enclosed region. If two regions share an edge, then we construct an edge between the corresponding vertices in $dual(G)$.

To finish the proof using this duality transformation, we need to show that given a path p in G, we have a path p' in G' that produces the same output as p. Say $p = v_1 \xrightarrow{e_1} v_2 \xrightarrow{e_2} \ldots \xrightarrow{e_{i-1}} v_i$, the equivalent path p' is $p' = \xrightarrow{e'_1} v'_1 \xrightarrow{e'_2=(v'_{e_1}, v'_{e_2})} v'_2 \ldots v'_{i-1} \xrightarrow{e'_i}$. The crucial realization is that an vertex v_j in p have its corresponding edge in p' as $e'_j = (v'_{e_{j-1}}, v'_{e_j})$. Using Figure 4.1 as an example, the path $(a, 1, b, 2, c)$ is transformed into $(a', 1', b'_{12}, 2', c')$.

Assuming G is using the Data State Model, and that G' is using the Data Flow Model, p in the functional notation gives $e_{i-1}(\ldots e_2(e_1(v_1))) = v_i$, and p' gives $v'_{i-1}(\ldots v'_2(v'_1(e'_1))) = e'_i$. Given that the vs in G are states that correspond to e's in G', we see that the inputs $v_1 = e'_1$ and $v_i = e'_i$ and the two paths gives same output. In the reverse case where G is the Data Flow Model and G' is the Data State Model, we can obtain the same output by the same principal. This is because the transformation shows that the order of processes and data states that p visits have exact equivalents in p'. Therefore, using this duality transformation, we can construct a data flow model that is *as-expressive-as* a given data state model, and vice versa. Hence, the two models are *equivalent in visualization expressiveness*.

QED.

3. Analysis of Characteristics

We have described the two visualization models, and how they are related to each other via its visualization expressiveness. Because of the different emphasis in expression, the two visualization models have resulted in very different visualization user interfaces. Data Flow Model based systems create modules that correspond to the process nodes, and data transferring mechanisms are created to connect the modules. On the other hand, Data State Model based system create data stores that correspond to the data states, with data processing procedures created to connect the data states. While the two models have the same expressive power in describing visualizations, here we discuss their different characteristics when utilized to implement a visualization system.

3.1 Data Flow Model and Data Flow Visualization Systems Analysis

There are several examples of visualization systems that manifest the data flow network model. AVS [103, 8], IRIS Explorer [54], and IBM Data Explorer [50] are some examples of such systems. As an user interface, all of these systems use a large canvas area where a palette of modules (nodes) can be placed. Users can then connect these modules to signal various connections. The focus of these systems is to enable the user to easily construct an scientific visualization process that visualizes the large data set.

The construction describes how the data flows through the system, which also describes the dependency of the various modules. For any given module to execute correctly, the corresponding inputs must be up to date. This means that the system must remember the state of each module so that the correct output will be generated. In addition, these visualization systems allow the association of interface widgets such as sliders with module input parameters.

Strength. The focus of these systems is to enable the user to easily construct an scientific visualization process that visualizes the large data set. The construction describes how the data flows through the system, which also describes the dependency of the various modules. For any given module to execute correctly, the corresponding inputs must be up to date. This means that the system must remember the state of each module so that the correct output will be generated.

The strength of these systems is that they are focused on getting the user from a data set to a visualization [43, 103] (see Figure reffig:avs-network). When the user has a particular kind of visualization in mind for her data set, she constructs a mental model of how to process the data into a visualized form. The data flow network model directly supports this user goal. The model bridges the "gulf of execution" by modeling the mental transformation the user performs to the data. This is extremely powerful, because the user can accurately and quickly construct a visualization that conforms to her mental image.

Weakness. The strength of the Data Flow systems is also its weakness. Because the user often must have a pre-existing notion of the visualization that she requires, the model supports the construction of the visualization pipeline but provides limited sup-

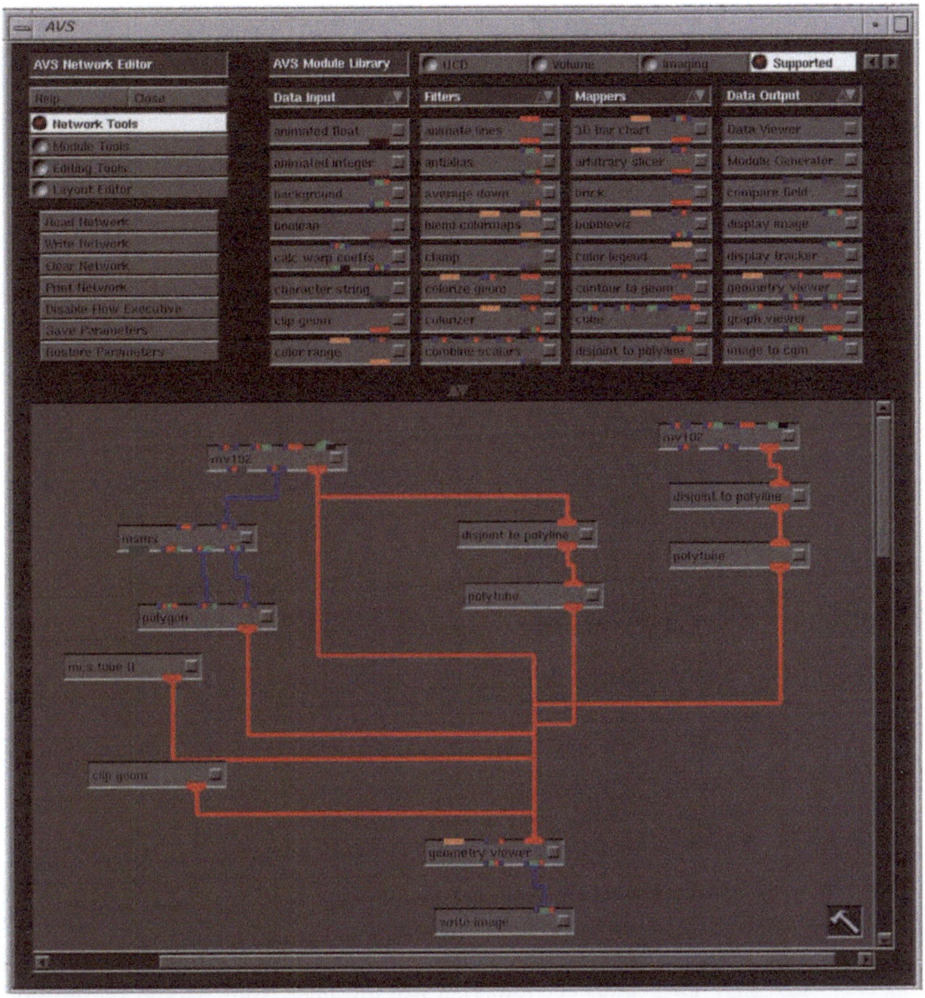

Figure 4.2. An example of a AVS Data Flow network that enables users to specify the visualization process of visualizing a molecule. Each operator is succinctly specified graphically.

port for explorations of the pipeline. For example, while you can have multiple views in AVS, you can typically only individually manipulate each view separately.

Moreover, these systems generally focus on the generation of a single visualization, instead of multiple visualizations of several different data sets. Its narrower focus on processes allows the easy construction of the visualization model, but also causes the screen spaces to be concentrated on the modules and their interconnections, which leaves very little screen space for the resultant visualization.

Also, because of the focus on single-view visualization, most Data Flow systems do not use the canonical form of the Data Flow Model as described in Section 1. That is, each edge in the model does not necessarily correspond to a single data state. This situation could lead to user confusion when two different data sets simultaneously use the same pipeline describing the same data visualization process, because they will not be able to individually examine the progress and status of these two data sets.

3.2 Data State Model Analysis

Data State Model based systems emphasize the operands rather than the operators in the system, and thus the user can more accurately gauge the intermediate results, and make adjustments during operation execution. They also make visible separate data states instead of data stages. Operations are generally specified either via a command macro script language, or via dialog boxes. Some interaction operations are manipulated directly, such as by using a mouse.

The application of operators automatically creates the dependency between visualization objects. The software system must also have an executive that keeps track of the state of each visualization object, and its inputs and outputs. To ensure correct output, the system executes the operators in the correct order to ensure dependencies are keep up to date.

An instantiation of the Data State Model is our Spreadsheet for Information Visualization system. Other similar spreadsheet systems such as Levoy's Spreadsheet for Images system [63] and IISS [44] have similar data transformation models. There have also been other systems that use the Data State Model but do not use a grid layout (e.g. NoPumpG [109], Forms/3 [108, 45], Fabrick [52]).

Strength. The strength of the systems that utilize the Data State Model is that they handle multiple data sets and data states extremely well, since the focus of the model is to represent data states. Each processing step in the transformation specified by the user can be visualized to view the intermediate results. The state model has advantages for some visualization tasks, because it makes the intermediate results explicit to the user, which enables the user to view intermediate results in planning later operations. This enables the user to monitor the progress of her task and how well the visualization is answering the questions posed by her study. For exploratory tasks, these intermediate results are important because they help the user in applying her intuition and experiences in the analysis of the data sets. Figure 5.6 shows how intermediate data states can be constructive in understanding inner and exterior of visual structures.

In the spreadsheet systems, tasks that deal with multiple visualizations are easier. For example, in Chapter 5, we show how a user can select an entire row of related visualizations and apply a single operator to all of them simultaneously. The parallel application of operators is very natural in the spreadsheet system, but awkward in the data flow system. The equivalent process in a data flow system requires dependency connections to be made between the modules manually. In the spreadsheet system, when the user selects an entire row, a temporary dependency is formed between the visualizations. As soon as the selection ends, the dependency is broken. Figure 5.8 illustrates an example of the parallel application of operators. An operation like this would be much more difficult to specify in a Data Flow system.

Weakness. The strength of the Data State system is also its weakness. It is a poor choice for tasks that do not require multiple visualizations on the screen at the same time. If a single view of the data suffices in a particular application domain, then a tailored task-specific visualization program should be used.

The construction of a single complex visualization is more difficult in the Data State paradigm than in the Data Flow systems. A traditional Data Flow system works better when the ability to specify complex operations using a point-and-click interface is important. This is because Data Flow systems tend to emphasize the operators needed to achieve a desired result, while the Data-State-based systems tend to emphasize the "what-if" exploration of the operands.

For example, in Data State systems, commands and scripts are typically used to specify how to construct an visualization, as in Figure 5.13. This is less visual and less intuitive than Data Flow systems.

3.3 Discussion

The value of the Data State Model is that it specifically represents the states from value to view, while Data Flow Model is more or less a "programming language" and is not concerned with such conceptual organizations but instead enable better descriptions of the visualization processing steps.

What does this analysis point us toward in the future? It's clear from our analysis so far that the two models are equivalent in their expressiveness, but the differences are highlighted when we consider the user interactions resulting from building one system using one model versus the other model. By focusing on process versus data, we can create dramatically different user interfaces.

The strengths and weaknesses mentioned above can be used as design guidelines. Situations that calls for direct specification of the visualization process should probably use a Data Flow Model, because it can help users to succinctly describe the process that is required to analyze their data. Situations that require serendipitous discovery and examination of intermediate data is best served by a Data State system that visualizes the data at each step of the process.

Finally, it is worth noting that a system combining both models could potentially be built. Each cell in a spreadsheet system using the Data State Model has a visualization process behind it. One could imagine a system where double clicking on the cell might bring up a Data Flow visualizer of the visualization process that can then be directly manipulated. The research challenge is in showing the user which cells will be affected by the manipulation of the Data Flow network. The interdependencies between the cells may be complex and this technique might not scale to large and complex networks.

4. Summary

Visualization can be viewed as a series of transformations that transcribes data values into graphical views. The relationship between view and value has been modeled primarily in two graphical models: Data Flow Model and Data State Model. The Data Flow Model has been well-established, especially in scientific visualization, and its capabilities and expressiveness is well-understood. Our main concern in this chapter is to understand, compare, and constrast the two models.

First, in this chapter, we proved that the Data State Model is equivalent in visualization expressiveness to the Data Flow Model, and vice versa, which means that we can model the same visualizations using either model.

Second, even though the two models are equivalent in expressiveness, we observed that their instantiation in the user interface gives each model different strengths and weaknesses. On the one hand, the Data State Model is well-suited for data and knowledge exploratory tasks. For example, the Visualization Spreadsheet system we built uses the Data State Model because the model naturally expresses the data states in the system, and shows intermediate results, which is important in exploratory tasks. The viewing of intermediate results in exploratory tasks is often important in the data and knowledge discovery process, especially in Information Visualization. On the other hand, the data flow visualization systems, such as AVS, uses the Data Flow Model and are suitable for the construction of a visualization process.

These advantages and disadvantages of each model should become more and more apparent in the future, and we hope this chapter have pointed some directions for future researchers to further understand the differences between the two models.

Chapter 5

THE VISUALIZATION SPREADSHEET ILLUSTRATED

The basic trick in user interface design is to find a starting place that is somewhat recognizable, and then help the user grow into the strongest set of tools possible.

—Alan Kay, 1998 CHI Conference Keynote Speech

The development of the Data State Model was inspired by the need to develop a general visualization system based on the spreadsheet paradigm. Spreadsheets are geared to allow users to examine the intermediate results carefully to form the next exploratory phase of the data analysis process. This chapter is designed to introduce the Visualization Spreadsheet concept and to illustrate the underlying principles that make up its power. The idea is to illustrate both the Data State Model and its concrete instantiation in the Visualization Spreadsheet.

So, in this chapter, we show the principles underlying the power of the visualization spreadsheet paradigm by presenting a set of scenarios and case studies of the usage of our visualization spreadsheet system in several data domains. We show how the Visualization Spreadsheet afford the construction of "what-if" scenarios, by applying different operations to the cells. We show how our system enables users to compare visualizations in cells using the tabular layout. Users can use the spreadsheet to display, manipulate, and explore multiple visual representations for their data. Just as a numerical spreadsheet enables exploration of numbers, a visualization spreadsheet provides a framework for exploring large and complex visual information. Structuring user interactions using a spreadsheet paradigm creates a powerful tool for information visualization.

First we discuss the research vision and plan for the Visualization Spreadsheet in 1 and 2. In Section 3, we describe the original molecular biology data domain that motivated our spreadsheet research. Then in Section 4, we describe other data domains used in our examples throughout the book. In Section 5 we use examples to illustrate a set of principles that make spreadsheets a powerful paradigm. In Chapter 6, we present a detailed case study of using the spreadsheet to analyze an abstract data set—the content, usage, and structure of a very large Web site. We show how the principles apply in this specific data domain.

Sections 3 and 4 are detailed descriptions of the data domains that are needed to understand all of the details in Section 5, but are not necessary for understanding the rest of the book. Also, Chapter 6 is an extended example of these principles, and is valuable, but not essential for understanding the rest of the book. Some readers may choose to skip the detailed description of the data domains and the detailed case study on web analysis, and read the essential Section 5 on illustrated principles.

1. Research Vision

Building a Visualization Spreadsheet poses a large set of research questions. This project addresses three types of key research questions. In Figure 5.1, we show an overview of the issues we studied while building a spreadsheet framework for visualization. At the high level (*High-Level Challenges*), the thesis explores the properties of applications, tasks, data, and visualization techniques that are suited to the spreadsheet paradigm. At the middle level (*Model Questions*), the thesis investigates the models needed to support three types of users: end users working with spreadsheet-based applications, application builders who assemble applications from defined components, and domain extenders who add support for new data types, visualizations, and operators to the framework. At the lowest level (*Core Objectives*), this thesis will examine core design and implementation issues including the key notions of data domains, cell values and views, operations, temporal mappings, and extensibility. Finally, the bottom box shows future related issues such as performance, collaborative spreadsheets, screen space, user interface, and visualization techniques.

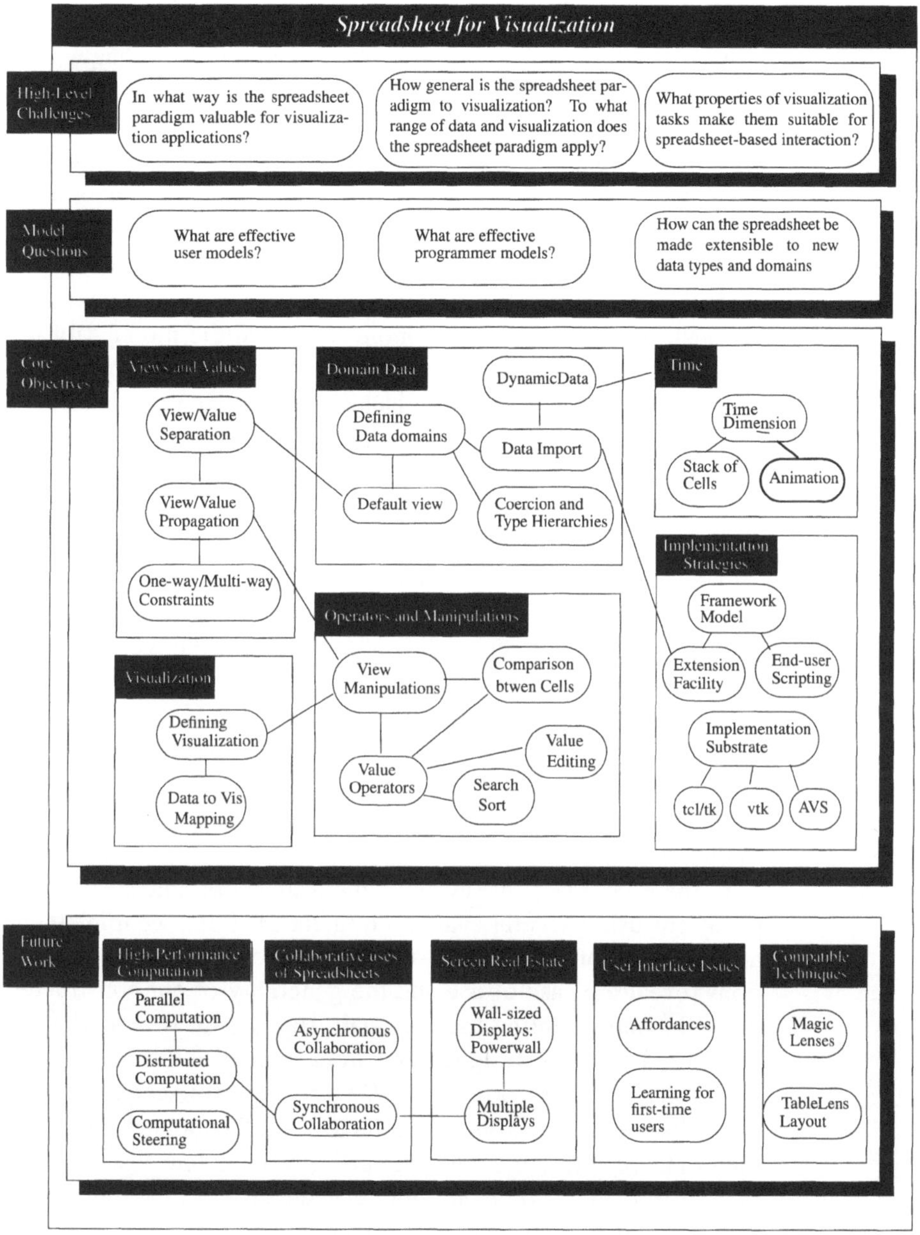

Figure 5.1. Grand Vision for Visualization Spreadsheet research. This figure shows an overview of issues involved in building a spreadsheet for visualization. The implementation of the *Core Objectives* enables us to answer the *Model Questions*, which in turn help us meet the *High-Level Challenges*. In creating this framework, the high-level challenges govern the formation of model questions and core objectives. In the bottom box, we show potential future research that is enabled by the examination of the core objectives.

2. Research Approach

In this section, we give an overview of our research plan, which is shown in Figure 5.2. We take a prototype-driven research approach in studying how spreadsheet environments can be employed for visualization. The plan encompasses three phases of the project — domain studies, design and implementation, and evaluation.

In the first phase, we perform domain-specific studies to gather user requirements. For each new domain, we also perform an initial interface design. We compare our design with other existing spreadsheets [63, 44] to gain more insight in the modularity required. We then put the experiences back into the construction of a general spreadsheet tool for visualization of dynamic data.

In the second phase, we perform an analysis of all requirements gathered in the first phase, and design and implement the spreadsheet framework. By gathering the requirements from these domain studies, we ensure the plausibility of the design for multiple data domains and visualization methods, which is one of the high-level challenges. Designing the interface for domain specific tasks helps us discover the properties of tasks that make them suitable for spreadsheet-based interaction. We then implement the Visualization Spreadsheet framework using the Tcl/Tk user interface building language [76] and the Visualization Toolkit (VTK) [92]. We chose Tcl/Tk because it is well-suited for building exploratory interfaces. VTK provide much of the functionality of existing visualization systems.

In the final phase, we evaluate the framework and specific applications using several evaluation methods. First, we implement applications for the domain-specific studies. The implementations reveal the ease of use and the generality of our constructed tool. By implementing these domain studies, we reveal whether the spreadsheet we designed and implemented in phase two can indeed handle these domains. We also perform scenario walk-throughs with specific domain tasks to see if the tool helps users in their data exploration goals. We further validate our visualization system framework by examining a wide variety of visualization techniques using our visualization model.

3. Original Data Domain: Genetic Sequence Similarity

Biological Sequence Analysis. Modern biology has evolved to the point where the underlying mechanisms of biological organisms can be understood by digging down to the genes that control

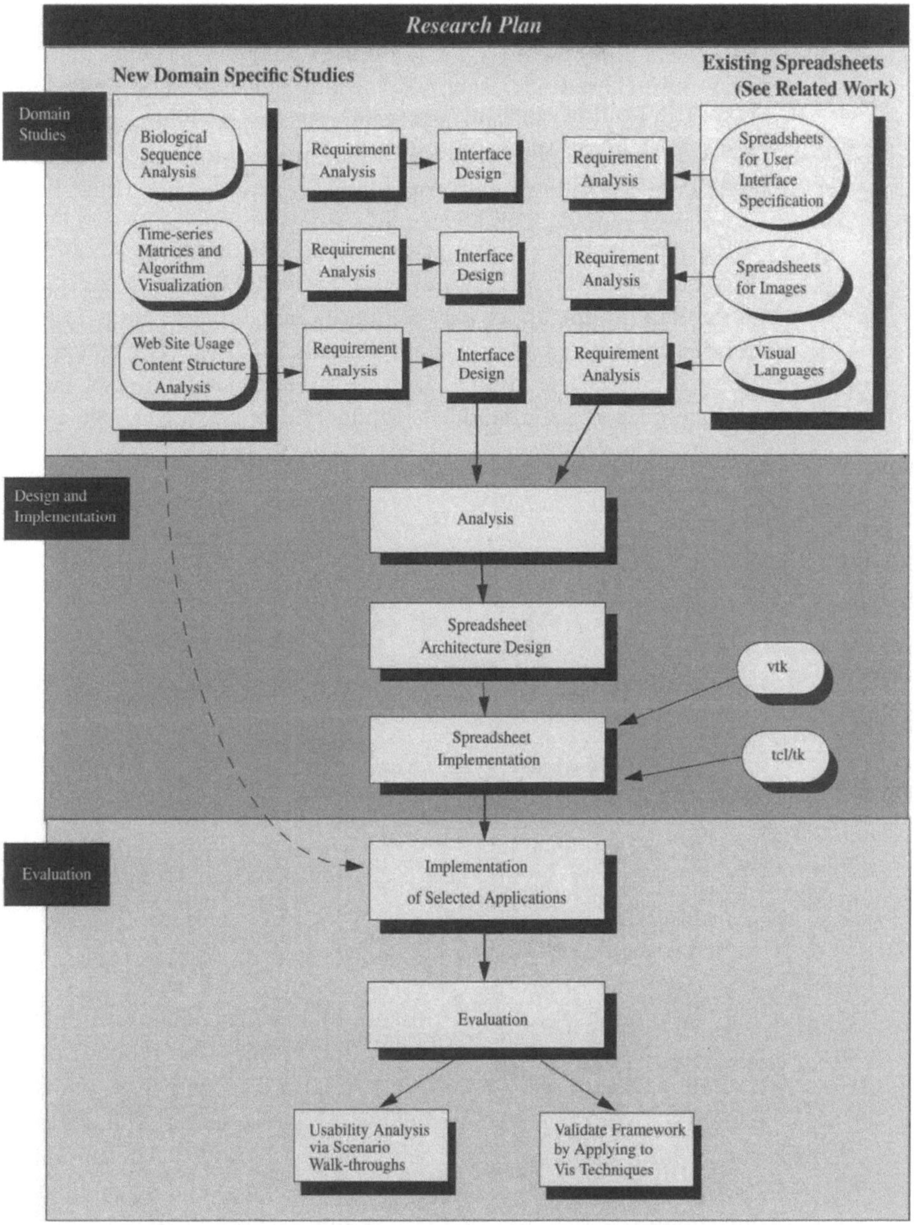

Figure 5.2. Research Plan for Spreadsheet for Visualization system. In the first phase, we perform domain specific studies to gather requirements. For each new domain, we also perform an interface design to capture interface requirements. In the second phase, we perform an analysis of all requirements gathered in the first phase, and design and implement the framework. In the final phase, we evaluate the framework and specific applications using several evaluation methods.

how cells function. These mechanisms play an important role in our lives. Indeed, our very existence depends on genes passed from one generation to the next, because the inherited genes encode the proteins that are necessary for our survival. These proteins fold in complex physical structures, which help to define their functions in the complex chemical reactions that occur in our body. Over many generations, the functions of the proteins in turn affect the encoding of the genes through the evolutionary mechanisms of mutation and natural selection. This four-way interaction is depicted in the upper part of Figure 5.3. Because organisms are related through evolution, genetic material from different organisms often share common functions. Molecular biologists seek to determine and understand the connections between these evolutionary relationships.

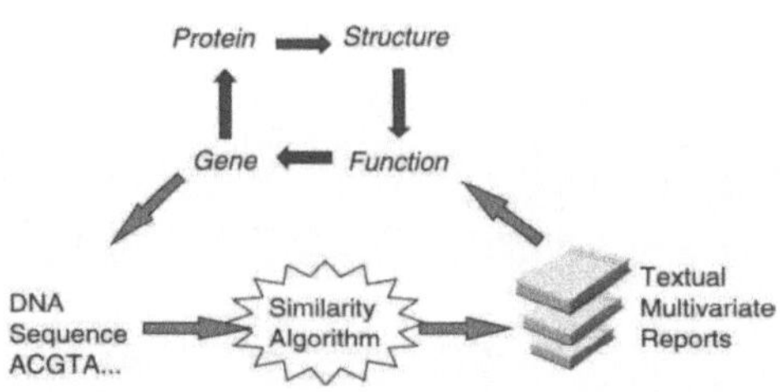

Figure 5.3. Molecular biology seeks to determine the interaction between gene, protein, protein structure, and protein function. Similarity algorithms provide a shortcut for finding possible protein functions for an unknown sequence.

Even though we already possess increasing amount of knowledge on this four-way interaction, the vastness of genetic information, the expensive labor-work required to gather it, and the expensive work required to analyze it have so far so far hampered our precise comprehension of molecular biology. Traditionally, painfully detailed lab experiments are designed and carried out to determine the function of the proteins. This is still a relatively slow process.

One method used to improve protein function determination is through sequence similarity analysis using computers—the comparison of a single sequence against the databases of known sequences. Sequence similarity algorithms are helping scientists to solve part of this puzzle by revealing the relationships between different genetic sequences. Sequence similarity algorithms are a well-developed aspect of computational molecular biology research and employ dynamic programming and heuristic search techniques. These algorithms identify similar regions (also called alignments) between sequences. These alignments provide clues to possible protein functions for the unknown input sequences, reducing the need for painstaking lab work [41]. The information that a computer provides in a few hours would otherwise take months of lab work.

Ironically, as more information about sequences becomes available, potentially reducing the need for laborious laboratory work, the task of analyzing the sequences on computers becomes increasingly difficult. BLAST [3] is one of the most popular similarity search algorithms in use today, but its running time is approximately proportional to the size of the database. In the past two decades, molecular biologists who conduct large-scale genetic sequencing projects are adding to the databases by using automated DNA sequencing machines. As molecular biologists discover new genes of various organisms and the functions of corresponding proteins, the information is being cataloged in the form of nucleic acid sequence databases for genes, and amino acid sequence databases for proteins. GenBank, the primary repository for DNA sequence data, contains roughly 499,000,000 nucleotides in 744,000 sequences as of April 1996, and is doubling every 1.3 years [72, 13]. The rate of increase will further accelerate as large projects such as the Human Genome Project [75] and the *Arabidopsis thaliana* Genome Project gain more momentum [99]. Even using computers, keeping pace with the analysis of these data is a difficult task for biologists.

This data domain has a number of properties similar to many datasets we encounter in information visualization: (1) The similarity reports are highly textual, and (2) the similarity relationships between items are an important visualization problem.

AlignmentViewer. We became interested in the Visualization Spreadsheet concept through our collaboration with molecular biologists who are interested in exploring plant DNA sequences. The biologists often compare a given sequence against a database of known sequences using similarity search algorithms, which produce reports indicating regions of similarity. These regions of similarity are also called "alignments". These reports can be hundreds of pages long for a single sequence. To help the biologists use these reports, we developed the AlignmentViewer system that visualizes the most prominent data [31, 32]. The following is a concise description of some of AlignmentViewer's features.

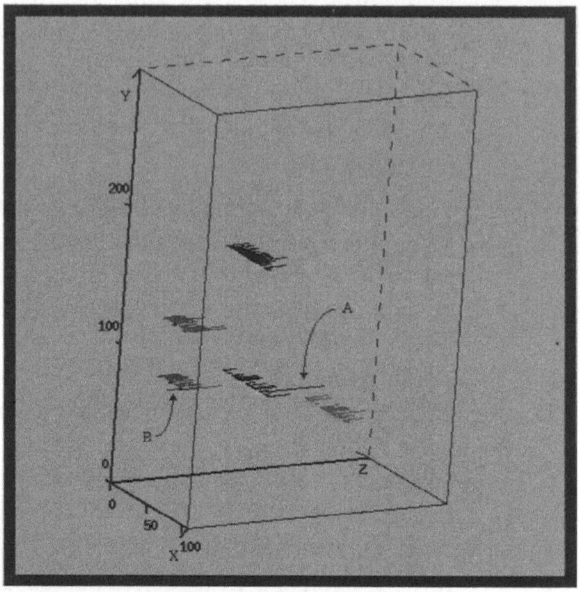

Figure 5.4. Several alignments represented in AlignmentViewer: X-axis is the position along the input sequence, Y-axis is the similarity score, and the Z-axis is the frame number of the alignment.

The basic 3D visual representation of this data consists of comb-like glyphs as shown in Figure 5.4 that show the different regions of similarity, the degree of similarity, and where the regions occur in the input sequence. Each alignment is associated with twelve variables, some of which are listed below:

- *Position.* The position in the input sequence where the alignment starts.
- *Frame*, or *frame number.* The frame number defines how the DNA sequence is translated into a protein sequence. DNA sequences are composed of a four letter alphabet. Three DNA bases encode one *protein residue* (also called an *amino acid*). A DNA sequence can encode a protein sequence starting from the first, second, or third position. The starting point determines how bases are grouped into residues. When comparing a DNA sequence to a protein sequence, each encoding is tried separately.
- *Similarity Scores* and *Residue Pair Scores.* Similarity algorithms such as BLAST compute the similarity score of each alignment [3]. For each pair

of residues in an alignment, BLAST looks up the entry in a *substitution matrix* and gets the *residue pair score*, which is a measure of the match strength. A positive entry corresponds to a good match, and a negative entry corresponds to a bad match [35]. BLAST then sums all residue pair scores in the alignment to obtain the similarity score.

An alignment also includes a matching vector. This vector, represented by an array of integers, contains the residue pair scores of the matches starting from the first matching position. Therefore, an alignment can be described by the above twelve variables, plus a matching vector.

AlignmentViewer uses three spatial axes and one temporal axis. Any of the twelve variables can be mapped to any of the four axes. The temporal axis allows the user to construct animations with respect to the temporal variable [32]. Within the 3-dimensional spatial image, the matching vector is represented by a comb-like glyph. The lengths of the teeth of the comb correspond to the integers comprising the matching vector.

The user can explore the data further by such means as interactively rotating, translating or scaling the representation, following a hyperlink to the textual report, mapping the data into a different geometric representation, animating the information over a variable, and filtering the data. The report data has many variables, and only a small number of them can appear in a single 3D visualization. AlignmentViewer mitigates this problem by enabling the user to selectively map the data dimensions onto 3D space, and allowing dynamic filtering of this data. In addition to dynamic query capabilities, we also support several types of animation along any of the dimensions, enhancing the display to 4D.

Motivation: Multiple Visualizations. Biologists found this visualization technique extremely useful in the discovery of biological artifacts [31, 32]. AlignmentViewer allowed them to find solutions to questions that were hard to answer, or questions that no one had thought of asking before. A large number of the questions involved the relationship between two or more similarity reports. The AlignmentViewer's visual representation enabled biologists to compare visualizations of related sequences, and the biologists found this ability useful. We noticed that the biologists often put two visualizations side-by-side on the screen to compare and contrast the visual features. They also frequently applied the same operation on two visualizations simultaneously, such as rotating to similar orientations, or applying animations to both at the same time. However, trying to do this simultaneously to two applications on the screen is difficult and cumbersome.

While our information visualization techniques provided biologists with the tool to view genome data in new and novel ways, a new paradigm was clearly necessary to take them to the next level of exploration. They have found the ability to compare visualizations for related sequences useful, and have specifically requested the ability to apply a number of different operations to the visualizations simultaneously. Our experience with the biologists motivated us to think about how we could support such behavior in a more general environment, where users can perform these tasks efficiently and productively.

First Spreadsheet: Spreadsheet for Similarity Report. Our first spreadsheet system called "Spreadsheet for Similarity Reports" (SSR) was built for visualizing genetic sequence similarity reports, which grew out of the AlignmentViewer system mentioned above. We collaborated closely with molecular biologists who can interact with us frequently. This allows us to directly support their information analysis tasks. This close collaboration has allowed us to directly capture many of the requirements of building a visualization spreadsheet for this data. For example, this spreadsheet uses direct manipulation controls with menus and buttons, which specifies particular operations to be performed on the data sets. It also includes a similarity processing engine that is used to generate similarity data on-the-fly. We discuss more details of this system in Section 5

4. Other Data Domains

After our first system, we built our general visualization spreadsheet system called "Spreadsheet for Information Visualization" (SIV, pronounced "sieve"). SIV is built on top of a multi-platform interpreted development system, especially utilizing Tcl/Tk [76] and VTK [92]. VTK provides an object-oriented architecture with many pre-built visualization modules.

In this section, we briefly describe these more information domains on which our test studies are based. Each of these domains will illustrate specific problems our research group encountered in information visualization analysis tasks. In Section 5 we will further demonstrate the usage of the systems in these domains, and at the same time, illustrate the principles behind how the spreadsheet paradigm facilitates information visualization tasks. By using a task-centered approach, we illustrate concretely the principles that underlie how the SIV Visualization Spreadsheet enables users to solve problems in information visualization.

4.1 Time-series Matrices

Besides similarity data, a time-series of matrices is another type of data that presents challenges of the type commonly encountered in information visualization. Two major difficulties arise in dealing with time-series matrices. The first difficulty is to identify differences in the matrix values between successive matrices. The second difficulty is that there are many visual representations that can be applied. For example, the "cityscape" representation shows the matrix values as 3D bars, whereas the "heatmap" representation show the values as colored tiles [101]. Different representations extract different features, so an easy way to view and explore these several representations simultaneously is needed. Fortunately, the spreadsheet environment deals well with these difficulties.

We encountered two matrix series in trying to solve problems with molecular biologists, who are interested in studying the effect of mutation and natural selections on genetic sequences. Natural selection accepts certain mutations, which result in the substitutions of one protein residue by another residue. For a mutation to be accepted, the protein usually must function in a similar way to the old one, presumably due to chemical and physical similarities. PAM (Point-Accepted Mutations) [35] and BLOSUM (BLOcks SUbstitution Matrix) [47] are two matrix series with each matrix representing substitution probabilities at a given evolutionary distance. The two matrix series were calculated from different sets of information sources. An element M_{ij} of a matrix specifies the relative probability that the amino acids i and j will be substituted after a given evolutionary interval. A positive entry specifies an accepted mutation that is more likely than random, whereas a negative entry specifies less likely than random.

The detailed nature of this series of matrices results in a large amount of information [35]. For example, biologists use these matrices in the calculation of similarity between sequences. Unfortunately, the computational molecular biology community have not applied visualization techniques to these matrices. To be sure, biologists want to understand the nature of these matrices because of their mathematical and biological complexity. The computational molecular biology community seeks to understand these matrices, because the choice of which matrix to employ is dependent on the situation. We have used the SIV system to try to gain a better understanding of these matrices.

4.2 Algorithm Visualization

A third domain we examined is algorithm visualization. In the past, algorithm visualizations have used animation techniques and sequential layouts to show successive steps. In Section 5, we show how a spreadsheet can be used to easily construct both animations and tabular layouts of steps for 3D Delaunay triangulation. We also show how we can utilize multiple visual representations to enhance the comprehensibility of the visualization. We use this algorithm as an example of how algorithm visualization can be supported in our Visualization Spreadsheet.

The algorithm generates 3D random points using random number generators, and then forms tetrahedra from the points using Delaunay triangulation. Delaunay triangulation has been used in scientific and information visualization domains to generate structures around points. 2D Delaunay triangulation is an optimal triangulation and has a number of interesting properties, such as maximizing the minimum angles. However, 3D Delaunay triangulation is much more complicated than 2D, and is a more complex algorithm. Even though the problem of 3D triangulation is well studied, it is still non-intuitive for many people. So visualization techniques can help in gaining better insights into the algorithm.

5. Illustrated Principles

In this Section, we will derive and define the principles of the Visualization Spreadsheet concept by demonstrating SSR and SIV in the context of three data domains as described above—genetic sequence similarity, time-series matrix visualization, and algorithm visualization.

5.1 Derive Comparison Data Sets

In the data exploration process, much user interaction involves applying operators to data sets. The Visualization Spreadsheet facilitates these interactions by letting users explore "what-if" scenarios in a structured environment. For example, users can copy and then modify the contents of a cell, or perform an operation on two cells and put the result in a third cell. Whereas the application of operators has largely been viewed as a sequential process in other environments, the spreadsheet environment is capable of supporting non-sequential spontaneous explorations.

The spreadsheet paradigm provides a simple interface for performing value operators that derive new data sets, such as subtraction and addition. Let's illustrate using the algorithm visualization example. Figure 5.5 shows an algorithm visualization of 3D Delaunay triangulation, which forms tetrahedra from a set of 3D random points generated using random number generators. Here the columns show the results of the algorithm after 5, 6, 25, and 50 steps, from left to right respectively. Row 1 shows the point set using 3D scatter plots. Row 2 shows the transparent tetrahedra after performing 3D Delaunay triangulation. Row 3 represents the tetrahedra using edges between vertices.

In this example, we show how the Visualization Spreadsheet can be used to quickly perform operations between successive steps of the 3D Delaunay triangulation. For example, by adding the geometric contents of cells together, the user can aggregate representations together to create new representations that show differences between the steps of the algorithm. For instance, the user now wishes to examine the intricate relationships between the different results from successive steps. To do this, she adds several cells together to form new visualization:

```
AddCell 4_1 3_2 3_1 2_2 2_1
AddCell 4_2 3_3 3_2 2_3 2_2
AddCell 4_3 3_4 3_3 2_4 2_3
```

The first command adds the geometric contents in cells `2_1`, `2_2`, and `3_1, 3_2` together and put the result into cell `4_1`. The other two commands follow the same pattern and generates results for cells `4_2` and `4_3`. The result of these operations are shown in Figure 5.6. The user sees that the difference between each successive step of the generation of the 3D random points produces a larger polyhedron. This prompts the user to issue an additional command to add all of the triangulations together to form a new visualization:

```
AddCell 4_4 3_4 3_3 3_2 3_1;
```

See Cell `4_4` in Figure 5.5 for the result of this command. The command adds the geometric contents in all of the cells in Row 3 and produces a single content and puts into the bottom-right cell `4_4`.

Cells `4_1`, `4_2`, `4_3` shows differences between steps of the algorithm. Cell `4_1` shows the difference between step 5 and 6,

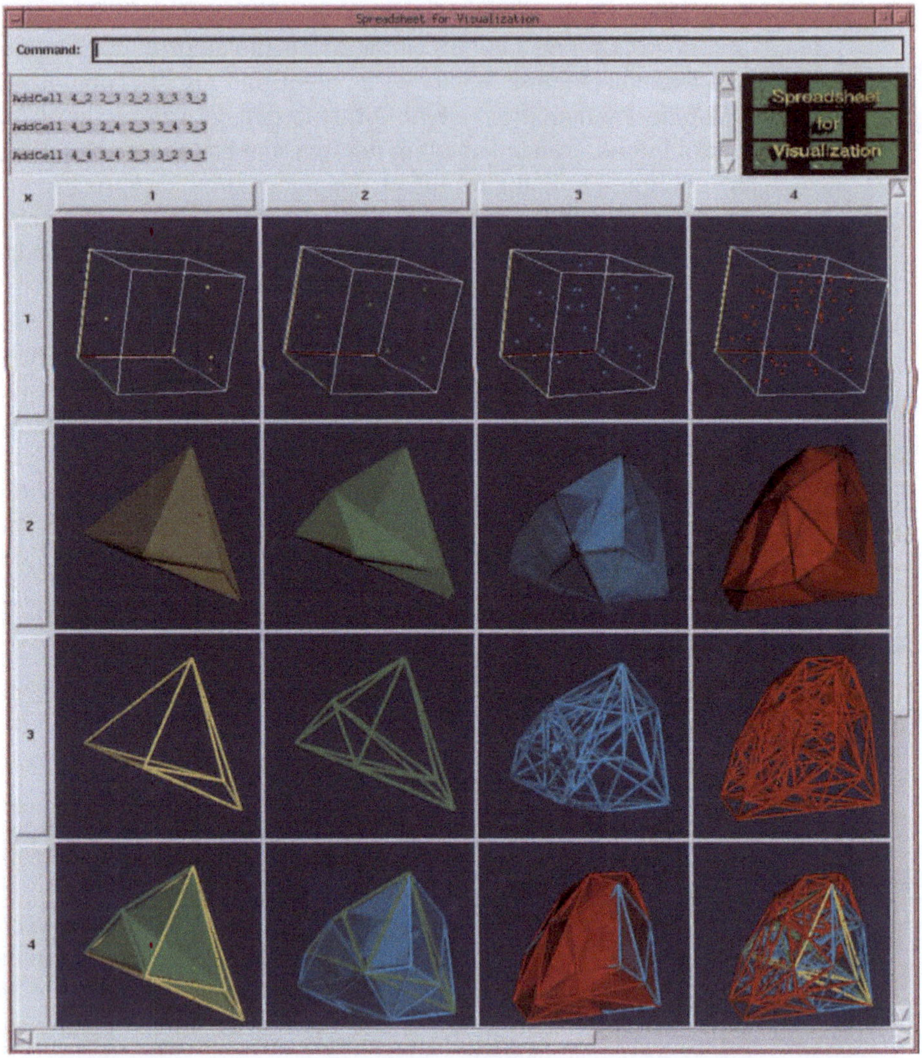

Figure 5.5. Visualization of 3D random point generation and Delaunay triangulation of the resulting point set. The columns visualize the outcome of the algorithm after 5, 6, 25, and 50 steps, respectively. The last row shows the result of several addition operations (the formula syntax is "`command` **result** *operands*".):

`AddCell` **4_1** *3_2 3_1 2_2 2_1*;
`AddCell` **4_2** *3_3 3_2 2_3 2_2*;
`AddCell` **4_3** *3_4 3_3 2_4 2_3*;
`AddCell` **4_4** *3_4 3_3 3_2 3_1*;

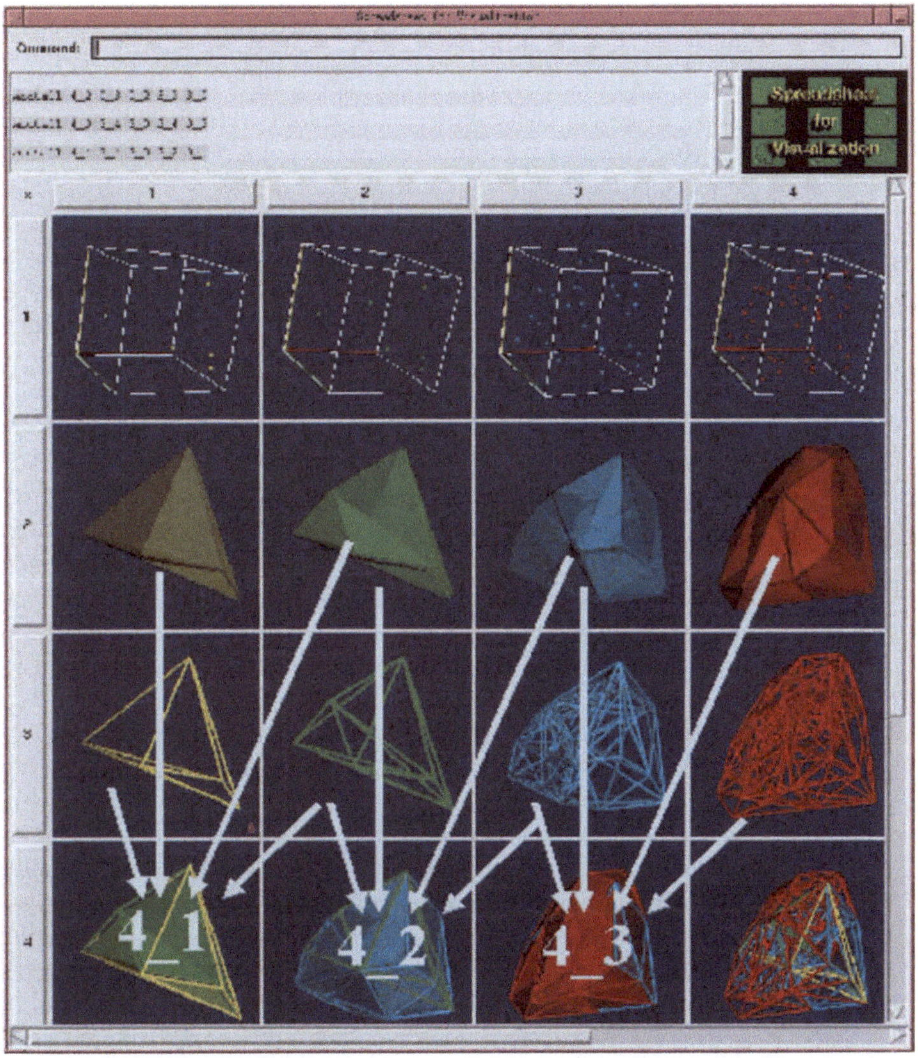

Figure 5.6. Generating cells 4_1, 4_2, and 4_3 in the Delaunay Triangulation example. Visualizing intermediate steps and then using addition to construct the final visualization in the understanding of 3D Delaunay Triangulation algorithm.

whereas 4_2 shows the difference between step 6 and 25. We can see where new points were added into the point set, as well as the structural changes in the convex hulls between steps. In Cell 4_3, we see the convex hull after 25 steps is almost completely embedded inside the convex hull obtained after 50 steps. We see the blue surfaces and vertices where the convex hull has not changed. Cell 4_4 shows the aggregate of adding all of the stick models in Row 3 together. These representations arise after many iterations of trying different combinations of the points, sticks, and surface representations of the data in Row 1, 2 and 3.

We see that each successive step indeed generates a larger and larger polyhedron. This discovery makes an observation about the Delaunay triangulation algorithm—with each additional point added to the set, we can only increase the size of the resulting triangulation, but not decrease it. This is a well-known result in computational geometry.

Interestingly, these algebraic operations can take on different semantics at multiple levels. At the low level, we can capture the cell images and perform image subtractions by subtracting corresponding pixels. At the mid level, as shown in the above algorithm visualization example, we can perform geometric object algebraic operations. We can define objects and algebraically add them to or subtract them from the scene. At the high level, we can perform algebraic operations based on the particular data domain semantics. See Figure 2.5 for an illustration of this concept.

We encountered the need to examine domain semantics for operators in the domain study with molecular biologists exploring DNA sequences. In the genetic sequence similarity data domain, the spreadsheet paradigm also provides a simple interface for performing operations such as data set subtraction or addition. Molecular biologists want to locate differences between several algorithm runs with different algorithmic parameters. In this example, the values are the sets of alignments, and we define two alignments to be equal if they share a region. Figure 5.7 shows a snapshot of an example session that is the result of a three step analysis:

Step 1 We load each column with data sets generated from the same input sequence by varying a parameter that is used to specify the sensitivity of the algorithm with respect to distantly-related versus closely-related sequences. We decrease the distance from far to near in columns 1, 2, and 3, respectively.

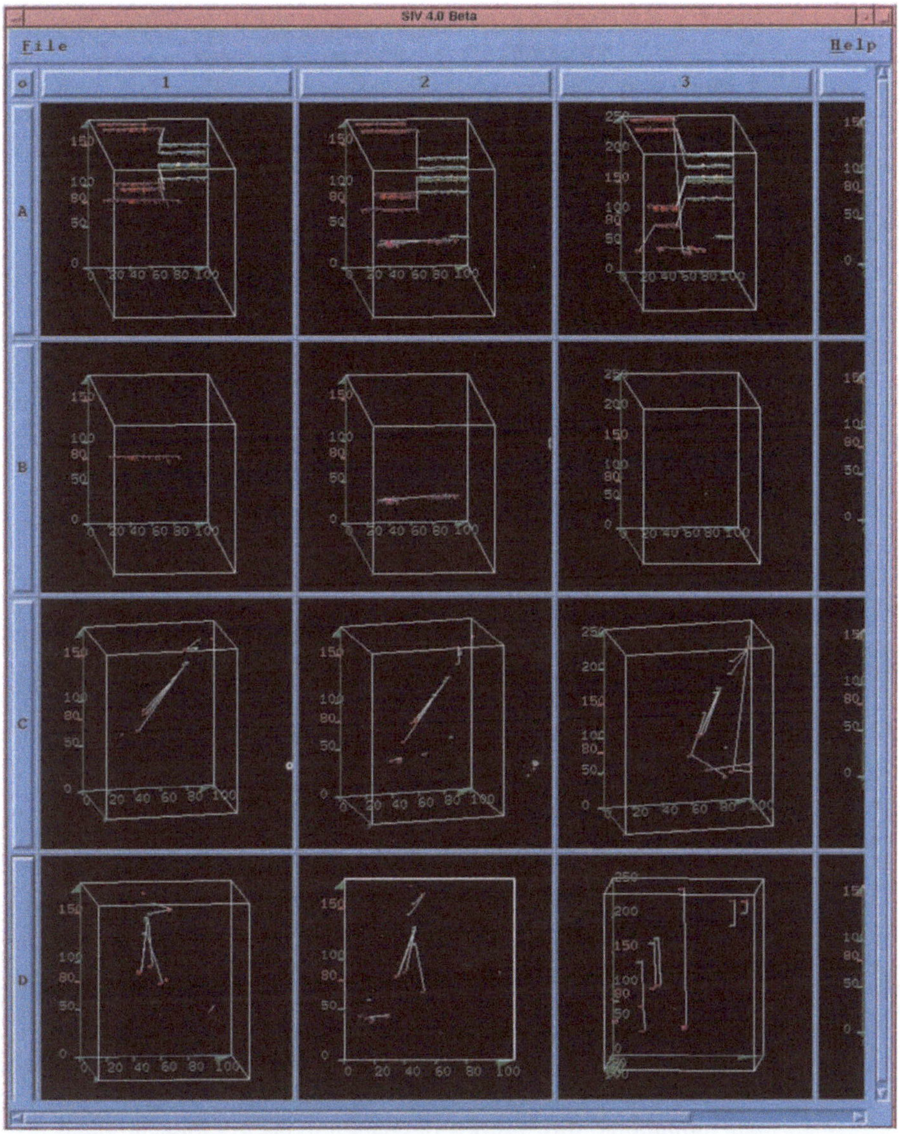

Figure 5.7. A screen snapshot of the Spreadsheet for Similarity Reports visualization system after performing three operations. (Step 1) Initially, we loaded each column with a slightly different, but related, dataset ($A1 = B1 = C1 = D1$, $A2 = B2 = C2 = D2$, $A3 = B3 = C3 = D3$). (Step 2) We selected Row B, and then subtracted cell $A3$ from it ($B1 = B1 - A3$, $B2 = B2 - A3$, $B3 = B3 - A3$). Cell $B3$ contains the empty set as expected. (Step 3) We changed Row C and D to show different views of Row A. The views show different sets of variables using a different representation, thus increasing our ability to see other dimensions of the multivariate datasets simultaneously.

Step 2 We select Row B and then subtract cell $A3$ from each cell in that row. Thus, $B1 = B1 - A3$, $B2 = B2 - A3$, $B3 = B3 - A3$. Cell $B3$ contains the empty set as expected. The cell values are alignment sets, and we define two alignments as equal if they share a region. Cells $B1$ and $B2$ show alignments found by using far evolutionary distance parameters, but not by the near used in $A3$.

Step 3 At this point, cells in Row C and D still contain the same data sets as the corresponding cells in Row A. We change the variables that are represented on the X, Y, and Z axis (the variable-to-axis mapping), resulting in different views of the datasets.

In this example, the visual subtraction allows the user to see the difference between the datasets.

Within the domain-specific semantic level, sometimes several possible definitions exists for the operator. For example, the difference operator above is only one of the three possible interpretations. We can actually define three different types of equality between alignments, resulting in three difference operators [30]. The three equalities are name, overlap, and exact. In name equality, two alignments are considered equal if they occur in the same database sequence. In overlap equality, the alignments must also share an overlapping region. In exact equality, the alignments must share the same exact region. Likewise, high–level algebraic operations in other domains should rely on the specific semantics of those domains.

With many data domains, the comparison operations are set algebraic rather than numeric. For example, instead of having negative numbers, we have the existence of set membership. An additional operator is set intersection. For instance, $A - B$ creates a new set of items in A except those that are also in B. In a numeric spreadsheet, negativity is often represented using a negative sign, coloring the item red, or putting the number inside of parentheses. For a task–specific operation in the Visualization Spreadsheet, we can define visibility, colors, or special icons to represent these different set memberships.

The ability to generate comparison data sets proves important in exploring the differences between related data sets. If we know the domain semantics, we can apply this spreadsheet principle to enable users to algebraically explore differences between data sets. The addition and subtraction operation shown here typify the case of comparing two similar, but not identical data sets, something of interest to researchers in many fields. The spreadsheet approach makes such algebraic manipulations straightforward.

> **Spreadsheet Principle 5.1** *Applying algebraic operators between cells* derives comparison data sets, *which enable comparison tasks to be carried out precisely in the Visualization Spreadsheet.*

5.2 Apply Operators in Parallel

One common, but equally important, interaction applies direct manipulation operations such as rotation, translation, and zooming. In a spreadsheet environment, often we want to be able to apply the same operation to multiple cells simultaneously. We have found this feature to be extremely useful for comparison tasks. For instance, the user can select the first row in Figure 5.5, then perform rotations simultaneously on all of the cells in that row, giving a rotationally–coordinated view of the data. Scatter plots in the same orientation provide correspondence between the points in different cells. Figure 5.8 illustrates an example of the parallel application of operators. This feature is useful in this situation because we want the pictures to be in similar orientations to provide correspondence between the points in different cells. In general, we have found the end user's parallel application of operators across cells extremely useful.

For example, in the time-series matrices example, understanding the differences between the matrices requires visually comparing a number of different matrices simultaneously. In Figure 5.9, the first, second, third, and fourth rows of cells visualize the PAM40, PAM120, PAM250, and BLOSUM62 matrix, respectively. Propagating view changes in parallel to multiple cells proved highly valuable in this data analysis situation. By selecting a row, we can compare the various visual representations in the same orientation. Alternatively, we can select a column and compare different matrices using the same visual representation.

Besides algebraic operators and simple scene operations, we have found that other operations, such as loading a data set, animating over a variable, and dynamic query filtering, are useful under this principle. For example, by selecting a column of cells, the user can apply an animation operation to those cells simultaneously. The animation tool provides accumulative, or sliced

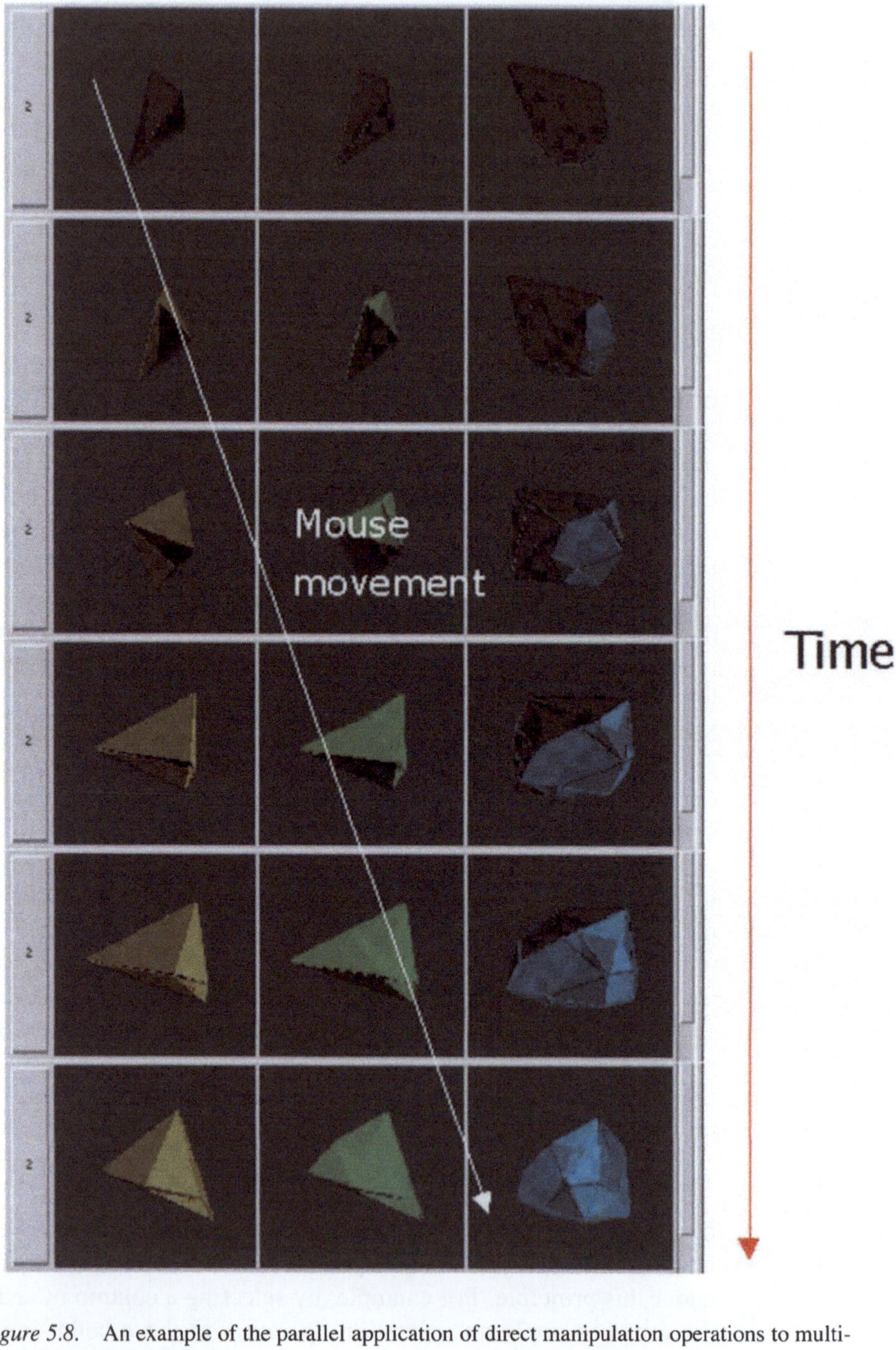

Figure 5.8. An example of the parallel application of direct manipulation operations to multiple cells simultaneously.

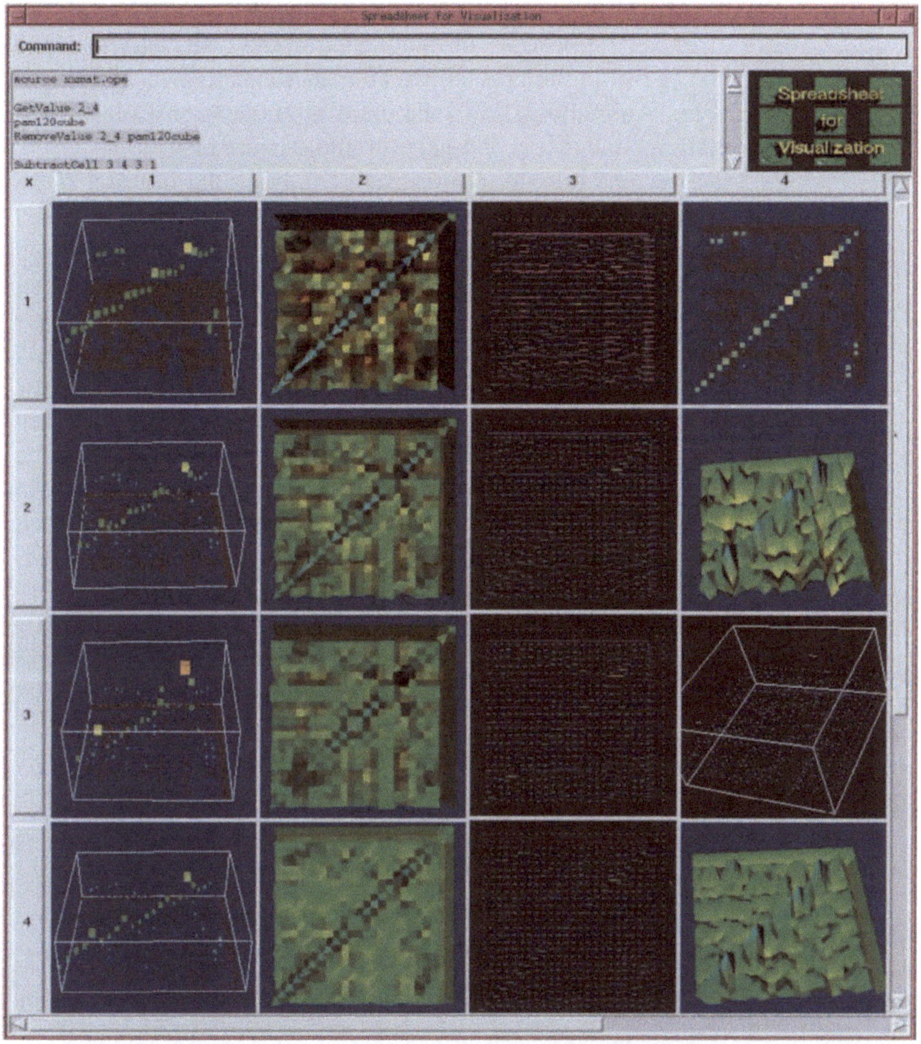

Figure 5.9. Visualization of time-series matrices using the Spreadsheet for Information Visualization system. The screen snapshot shows visualizations of protein residue substitution probability matrices of various evolutionary distances. The first, second, and third rows visualize matrix 40, 120, and 250 from the PAM matrix series. The fourth row visualizes matrix 62 from the BLOSUM matrix series. The first column uses a cube representation that maps positive matrix values to the volume, height, and color attributes of the cubes. The second column uses a carpet plot that maps values to the height and color of a 3D surface. The third column uses a bar representation that maps values to the length, height, and color attributes of the bars. The fourth column shows various representations in different rotational configurations.

animation over any variable [32]. A synchronized animation can be performed on a group of cells simultaneously. In Figure 5.7 for example, suppose we are interested in the distributions of the lengths of the alignments, so we animate the cells over the length variable. Animation shows the extra alignments in Cell $A2$ are short alignments when compared to the alignments in $A1$.

As another example, the user can apply a data filtering operator across a row of data to cut out unwanted data points. As a concrete example, in Step 1 of our sequence similarity example in Figure 5.7, we parallelly load the data sets by first selecting a column by clicking on the column button, and then applying a load-dataset operator to all the cells in that column. In Step 2, we parallelly subtract Cell $A3$ from Row B by first selecting Row B and then applying a subtraction operator to all the cells in that row. A filtering tool enables the user to explore subsets of the data. When the user interactively adjusts sliders controlling each variable, the view is updated in real-time. Using the filtering tool, closer inspection reveals that the short alignments in $A2$ are between 11 and 29 residues long.

Distributing a single operation across a group of data sets is a common interaction in data exploration. We speed up users' tasks by automating the chore of applying operations to a large number of cells.

Spreadsheet Principle 5.2 *The Visualization Spreadsheet easily affords* applying operators in parallel *to a large group of cells and data sets.*

5.3 Extract Multiple Visual Features Simultaneously

Users of the spreadsheet can also use the spreadsheet to compare different visual representations. For a given data type, we can often choose from many different visual representation techniques. Often, a technique contributes to the finding of one visual feature, while another visually extracts a different visual feature. Fortunately, the spreadsheet environment assists in the organization and display of various visual representations. Because our system can be easily extended to handle new techniques via command modules, it allows us to quickly experiment with and compare several representation techniques. Here we illustrate this flexibility in all three data domains.

The algorithm visualization of Figure 5.5 shows several different visual representations of a 3D Delaunay Triangulation. Row 1 represents the point set as 3D scatter plots, showing the spread of the points quite well. Row 2 shows the same data using transparent tetrahedra after 3D Delaunay triangulating the point sets. Through interactive rotation, this representation gives a better view of the relative placement of the points. It also shows the convex hulls of the point sets, and how the hulls change between steps of the algorithm. Row 3 represents the Delaunay triangulation as edges rather than tetrahedra, thus giving a better view of the interior structure of the triangulation.

Our SSR sequence similarity spreadsheet also allows changing of visual representation via a mapping tool. In Figure 5.7, the cells in Row C and D contain the same data sets as the corresponding cells in Row A, but we changed the mapping in Row C and D to show different variables of the similarity report. In this organization, the cells in a given column represent the same value; however, each row offers a different view of the data. The ability to map different variables to different axes in different cells improves a user's ability to see more variables simultaneously. In this spreadsheet, a click-and-point interface controls the operations. The user loads the columns with data one column at a time, and changes the mapping of the data of each row using the mapping tool dialog box. We implemented the mapping tool as a pull-down menu for each axis.

Exploring multiple features is also important in the domain of time-series matrices. By constructing several modules for different visual representations of matrices, we used our spreadsheet to answer specific scientific questions on the amino acid substitution time-series matrices. In Figure 5.9, the tabular layout shows different visual representations in different columns. The values in the cells are the same across each row, but we varied the visual representation to bring out different features of the data set.

We discovered several novel patterns in these matrices. In Figure 5.10, the first column uses a cube representation that maps positive matrix values to the volume, height, and color attributes of the cubes. This representation shows the interesting variation of the diagonal entries more clearly than the other representation methods. The entry represented by the orange cube varies more than any other entry.

The second column uses a "carpet plot" that maps values to the height and color of a 3D surface (using a rainbow colormap with

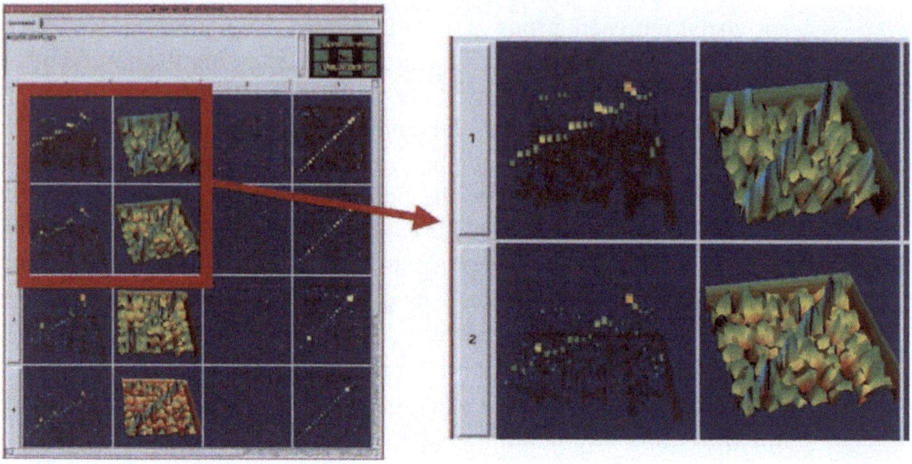

Figure 5.10. Discovering novel patterns using multiple visualization representations in the time–series matrices example.

negative entry mapped to red). The carpet plot technique shows that the matrices have different ranges of values (the colors get brighter and brighter from top to bottom).

The third column uses a bar-plot representation that maps values to the length, height, and color attributes of the bars. The bar-plot technique makes comparing a specific entry from matrix to matrix easy, and shows the overall decreasing trend of most off-diagonal entries.

Our experience shows the elegant organization of the spreadsheet allows interesting combinations of different visual representations of the underlying data. Users can compare and visually extract different features from the different representations. The spreadsheet environment equips users with the necessary tools to explore the representation space.

Spreadsheet Principle 5.3 *Users can represent data sets using several different visualization representation techniques, which enable them to* extract multiple visual features simultaneously.

5.4 Create Analysis Templates

The spreadsheet enables users to create templates to reliably repeat often-needed computations without the effort of redevelopment or coding. This advantage—evident in numerical spreadsheets—translates easily into visualization spreadsheets. Users can construct their own layouts in situations that programmers cannot foresee, and re-use them over and over again. By allowing users to enter data into cells in various configurations, the spreadsheet supports a variety of different tasks. This single easily understood, easily configured tool can handle multiple situations. Users, already familiar with tables, can immediately start organizing their data in this spreadsheet metaphor. For example, for easy comparison in numerical spreadsheets, users often put two numbers next to each other or load two sets of numbers into adjacent columns. Similarly, in the Visualization Spreadsheet, users layout two data sets next to each other, or compare two groups of data using adjacent columns. This flexibility contributed to the numeric spreadsheets' success.

For example, in Figure 5.7, the user set up a particular organization that enables the immediate detection of differences between different but related data sets. Each vertical column contains a different dataset generated by changing one parameter of the algorithm—the sensitivity of the algorithm with respect to distantly-related versus closely-related sequences. For example, even viewers without molecular biology training can see the similarity in the data sets' general structures, but also that some alignments that are present in cells $A2$ and $A3$ do not appear in $A1$. This example shows that the tabular organization of the spreadsheet enables the user to detect differences between visualizations of several datasets. Users can now take advantage of their visual comparison abilities to detect differences between data sets.

As another example, the columns and rows of the table increase the number of dimensions we can see simultaneously. In Figure 5.5, the columns show several snapshots of the steps of the 3D Delaunay algorithm. The columns show the results of the algorithm after 5, 6, 25, and 50 steps, from left to right respectively. So in this case, the columns are used to represent the time dimension. With the same analysis template, the user can analyze several different runs of the algorithm, examining a different random point generator each time.

Figure 5.9 demonstrates an analysis template of different visual representations set up for visualizing a series of matrices. Simply applying other matrix values to the cells enables multiple analysis. Configuring the spreadsheet lets us see how templates can be adapted to a wide variety of tasks, such as showing the time dimension, different data sets, or different visual representations.

As the above examples show, the tabular layout's flexibility lets users construct different analysis templates for different tasks, and thus contributes to the power of spreadsheet–based environments. Spreadsheets are familiar, flexible, easily configurable, and excellent for interactive comparison tasks. Coupled with the capability of simple direct manipulation operations that can be applied in parallel, we see how users can tailor the spreadsheet to individual situations on-the-fly.

Spreadsheet Principle 5.4 *The Visualization Spreadsheet enables users to perform repetitive analysis tasks by* creating analysis templates *that can be applied over and over again.*

5.5 Update Automatically via Dependency Links

One of the spreadsheet's advantages is that it automatically updates the contents of the cells based on the data dependencies between them. Now that the cells store complex data sets that may be composed of several different data sets of several different types, the dependency between cells is much more complicated than in the numeric spreadsheet. In SIV, since all objects are results of the application of an operator, the application of operators also specifies the dependency relationships between objects in the cells. This is consistent with the way numeric spreadsheets derive their dependencies between cells.

Each operator has input data ports and output data ports. Upon the specification of the application of an operator, the output data becomes dependent upon the input data.

In the Delaunay triangulation example, the dependency graph is shown by the flow chart in Figure 5.11. The figure summarizes the dependency relationships between the cells in this example. A point addition operator specifies the relationships between the cells in the first row. Corresponding cells in the first row are related to cells in the second and third row via a Delaunay triangulation operator. Cells in the fourth row are related to cells in the

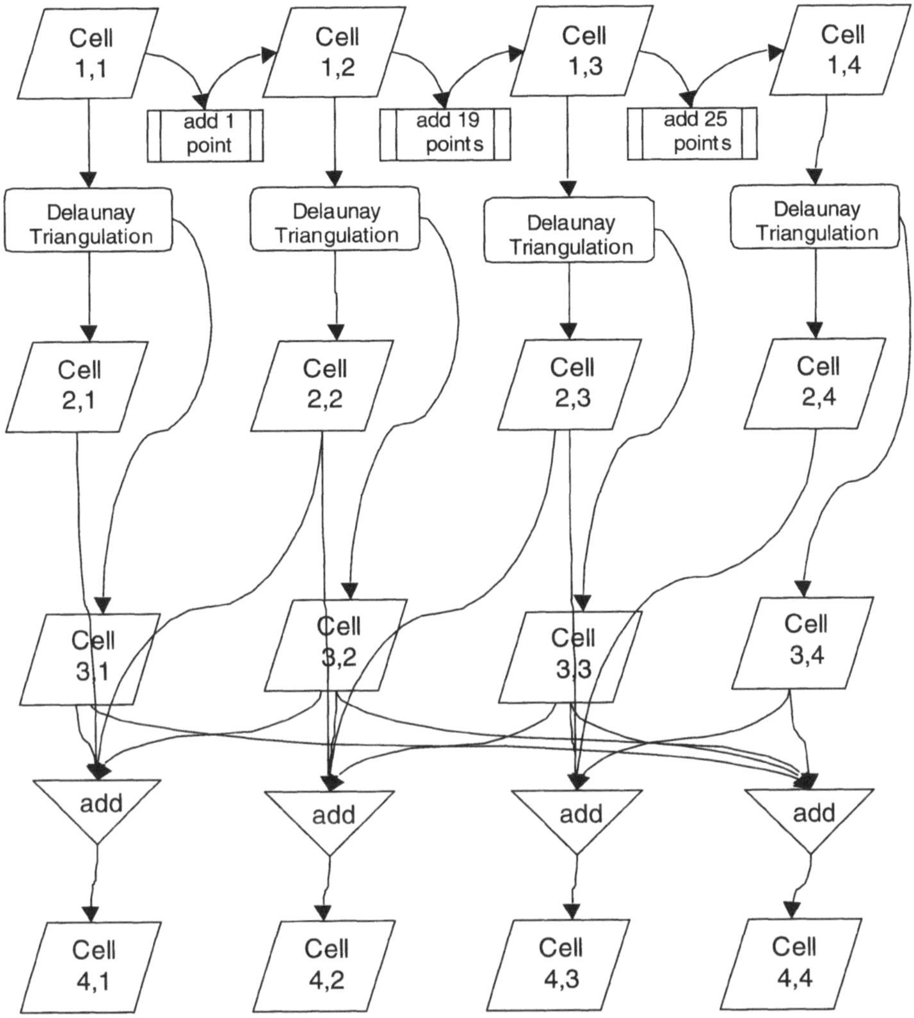

Figure 5.11. The Delaunay Triangulation Algorithm Visualization Dependency Flow Chart

third row by the geometric addition operator. For example, cell `4_4` is related to cells in the third row via an addition operator.

In the operation of the spreadsheet, the system keeps these declaration of dependency relationships in memory. Whenever the system notices a change in a cell that affects other cells, the system executes the corresponding commands that formed the dependency relationship to keep the relationship up-to-date. For instance, as Figure 5.11 shows, adding a single point in Cell `1_1` will cause Cell `1_2`, `1_3`, `1_4` to obtain an extra point in their data set as well. All other cells' content depend on this first row and thus will also be recomputed. By enabling the system to automatically keep these data sets up-to-date, we take away this burden from the user, which enables them to focus more on the analysis of the data sets.

An open problem is that these dependency relationships can become opaque to users, because they are not explicitly represented on the screen. Animation techniques may partially ameliorate this problem [51].

> **Spreadsheet Principle 5.5** *Visualization Spreadsheet* updates automatically via dependency links *between cells. Automatic recomputation based on dependencies among cells reduces the burden of computation on the user.*

5.6 Mapping Value to Structure using Custom Layouts

The advantages of the tabular layout are that it is familiar, flexible, easily configurable, and excellent for interactive comparison tasks. It can be tailored to multiple situations in a single tool that is both easy to understand, as well as easy to configure.

We used our SIV system to compare the two matrix series (PAM and BLOSUM). To understand the differences between the matrices, it is important to be able to visually compare a number of different matrices simultaneously. We found being able to quickly bring in data and lay them out in different ways to be extremely useful. For example, after 7 lines of commands, the last row shows the BLOSUM62 matrix. In Figure 5.9, the first, second, third, and fourth rows of cells visualize the PAM40, PAM120, PAM250, and BLOSUM62 matrix, respectively. In the horizontal dimension of the spreadsheet, the columns show the matrices using various visualization techniques.

By vertically scanning the spreadsheet, the user can detect differences between matrices quickly. The spreadsheet allows a way of comparing somewhat similar entries. Since the data is complicated, the spreadsheet furnishes ways to organize and compare matrix values across different matrices. As we can see from all the columns, the diagonals of these matrices have strong values, which makes sense since the identity substitution (no mutation) is favored by evolution. From the second column we see that the matrices are quite different because the colors get brighter and brighter from top to bottom. The last row shows the BLOSUM62 matrix, and we see its values are clearly different from any of the PAM matrices shown.

The tabular layout is one of the reasons why spreadsheet-based environments are so powerful. The organization is familiar to users, and simple direct manipulation operations can be used to rotate contents in the cells. It can be custom tailored to individual situations on-the-fly.

One important lesson learned from this example is the importance of being able to map values onto the structure of the spreadsheet. By using the vertical dimension of the spreadsheet for time and the horizontal dimension for various representation methods, we externalize the variability of the two variables we are interested in correlating. Without the spreadsheet, correlating between these two features visually is difficult. We call this the process of *Value to Structure Mapping*. By employing external cognition, we reduce the cognitive load of the user, and speed up the sensemaking analysis.

> **Spreadsheet Principle 5.6** *The Visualization Spreadsheet can* map value to structure using custom layouts, *which externalize the variability of variables using the horizontal and vertical dimensions of the Visualization Spreadsheet.*

5.7 Use Both Direct Manipulation and Textual Commands

How to access and apply operations is an important aspect of the Visualization Spreadsheet. We examined two different methods for performing spreadsheet operations.

The first method is a direct manipulation interface corresponding to a "noun-verb" model, where the user first selects a group of cells (the noun), and then applies an operation (the verb) to those cells. The operation is specified using a combination of menus and dialog boxes. For example, to set up the similarity data in Figure 5.7, the user first selects a column of cells, then performs a single import operation of a large dataset into those cells. Some example menus and dialog boxes used in SSR system is shown in Figure 5.12.

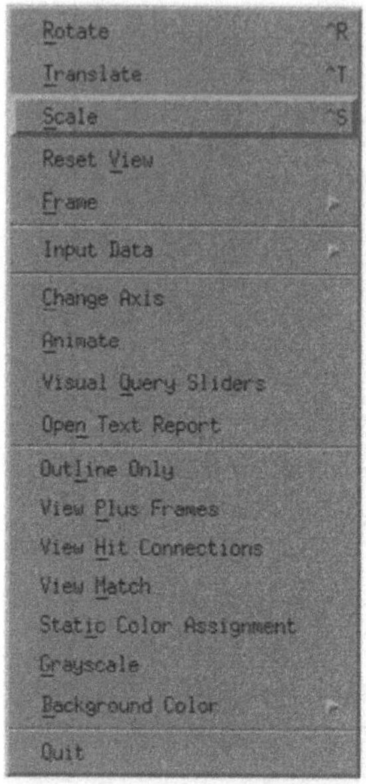

(a) Main popup menu

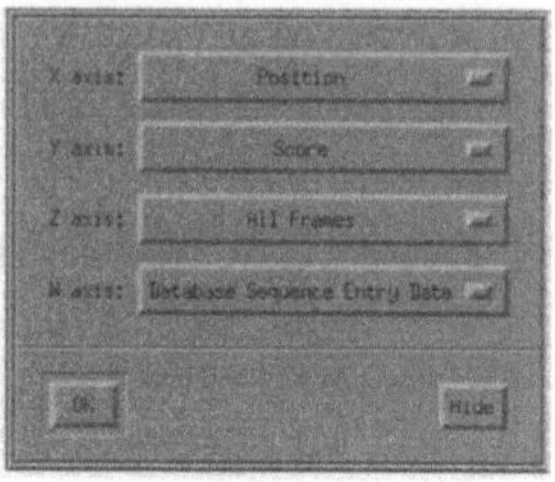

(b) Mapping dialog box

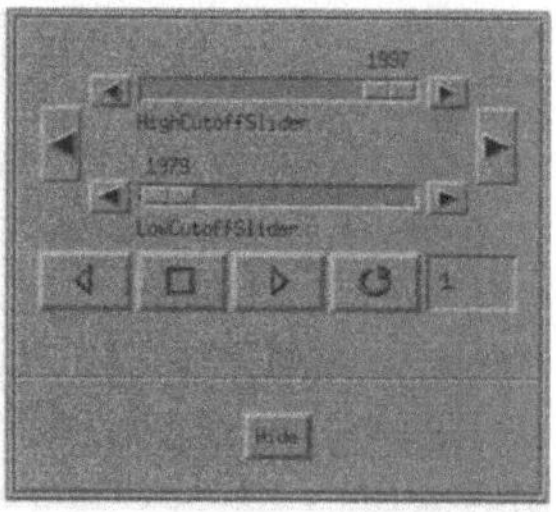

(c) Animation dialog box

Figure 5.12. Our Spreadsheet for Similarity Reports (SSR) visualization spreadsheet uses a direct manipulation interface with menus and dialog boxes, which makes the system easy to use.

The second method is a command and script language based interface. The user can interactively enter commands in an entry box, similar to a traditional numerical spreadsheet. Alternatively, she can write a script file and load in the script. For example, she can define a layout by writing a script that specifies the datasets and the representation method used for each cell. The script file can contain other non-layout commands such as animation, or even define new commands. In Figure 5.9, we can see in the history window, the user has just loaded a script with a predefined layout. An example of how commands and scripts are used is shown in Figure 5.13.

The command language can also be used to define modules to extend the spreadsheet, such as file input modules or modules that define a visual representation for a given data type. To use the module, the user simply loads the module, and the new commands

```
MathRandom3D pset4 100 50;

→ Scatter sca4 pset4 $red 0.05 1.0;
AddValue 1_4 sca4 axesActor;

→ Delaunay3D tri4 pset4 $red  0.5;
AddValue 2_4 tri4;

→ TubeEdge tube4 deltri4 $red;
AddValue 3_4 tube4;
```

Figure 5.13. Textual commands allow users to specify operations in the SIV spreadsheet using simple macro languages. Scripts can be specified in a file and loaded.

in that module become available to her. For example, in Figure 5.9, the user programmed new modules that implement new visual representations for matrices using the command language. The command language we defined for the visualization spreadsheet includes operators such as `SubtractCell`, `Scatterplot`, `ReadBioMatrix`, and `Carpetplot`. The operators follow the language convention: "`command result arguments`", where `command` operates on the `arguments` and puts the outcome in cell `result`.

From our experience of the two systems, we believe a combination of the two approaches is appropriate for the Visualization Spreadsheet. The advantages of a menu-based interface are that it is relatively intuitive to use for first-time users, and training time for new users is short. However, because there are many features in a visualization spreadsheet system, there is the danger of creating a large number of menus with no structure to them. Menu systems also tend to slow down expert users. The advantages of a command language based interface are its flexibility and its appeals to power users. Command languages can also be used to construct macros so complex tasks can be performed rapidly. The disadvantages are that command languages are difficult to master and require substantial training and memorization.

Spreadsheet Principle 5.7 *Visualization Spreadsheet should* use both direct manipulation and command languages. *For certain operations, one technique may be more appropriate than the other.*

6. Summary

We illustrated the principles behind how the spreadsheet paradigm facilitates information visualization tasks. Here we presented our system called Spreadsheet for Information Visualization (SIV, pronounced "sieve"). We presented specific examples while noting a number of issues and capabilities of our system.

We list the visualization spreadsheet principles in Table 5.1. With Principle 1, we illustrated how the visual spreadsheet paradigm facilitates data exploration by enabling researchers to derive comparison data sets using operators such as set addition and subtraction. In Principle 2, we illustrated how the spreadsheet paradigm enables the parallel application of operators to a range of cells, facilitating visual comparison of values in the cells. In Principle 3, we discussed how to use the spreadsheet paradigm to enable the exploration of multiple visual features in the spreadsheet simultaneously. This is especially useful in information visualization, since there are several different visualization representation techniques available at the user's disposal for a given data type. In Principle 4, by constructing a layout configuration, we showed that the user can set up analysis templates to apply to many data sets. In Principle 5, we showed how automatic recomputation based on cell dependency reduces the computation burden on the user. In Principle 6, by equipping users with a set of operations, we show that the Visualization Spreadsheet lets them explore data sets in their unique situations by mapping values to structures. In Principle 7, we show that direct manipulation and command languages should both be used in the Visualization Spreadsheet.

Principle 1	Applying algebraic operators between cells *derives comparison data sets*, which enable comparison tasks to be carried out precisely in the Visualization Spreadsheet.
Principle 2	The Visualization Spreadsheet easily affords *applying operators in parallel* to a large group of cells and data sets.
Principle 3	Users can represent data sets using several different visualization representation techniques, which enable them to *extract multiple visual features simultaneously.*
Principle 4	The Visualization Spreadsheet enables users to perform repetitive analysis tasks by *creating analysis templates* that can be applied over and over again.
Principle 5	Visualization Spreadsheet *updates automatically via dependency links* between cells. Automatic recomputation based on dependencies among cells reduces the burden of computation on the user.
Principle 6	The Visualization Spreadsheet can *map value to structure using custom layouts*, which externalize the variability of variables using the horizontal and vertical dimensions of the Visualization Spreadsheet.
Principle 7	Visualization Spreadsheet should *use both direct manipulation and command languages.* For certain operations, one technique may be more appropriate than the other.

Table 5.1. The Visualization Spreadsheet Principles

Chapter 6

DETAILED CASE STUDY: WEB ANALYSIS VISUALIZATION SPREADSHEET

A rigorous definition of the components of the information, specifying their number, level, and length, must procede any graphic construction.

—Jacques Bertin [14, p. 171]

In this Chapter, we present a detailed case study of using the spreadsheet to analyze a large abstract data set—the content, usage, and structure of a large Web site. We demonstrate how the visualization principles apply in this specific data domain.

1. Visualization of Web Space

Site administrators want to know patterns of use for their Web sites, so that improvements can be made. Strategists would also like to mine information about users, such as product interest. Users need tools to navigate and locate information faster. To support these sensemaking tasks, visualization of large hypertext spaces has been done by various researchers [5, 7, 27, 46, 111, 80, 71]. These systems are designed with a fixed priori with a limited set of tasks in mind.

A system has yet to provide a set of primitives for conducting iterative and cyclic analysis tasks on Web ecologies. In our work, we provide such a system by handling very large Web sites (15,000 files) and their associated evolving attributes [28].

We develop the use of the spreadsheet paradigm for visualization in the sensemaking of Web sites. We present a visualization application called the Web Analysis Visualization Spreadsheet (WAVS) using the spreadsheet paradigm that enables the processing and subsequent understanding of evolving Web content, usage, and topology (CUT). We use developed visualization techniques such as the Disk Tree [28] and Cone Tree [87] to reduce the cost of doing cyclic analysis tasks over hypertext document collections. For the purpose of this paper, we will examine the application of WAVS to the evolving Xerox Web site over a one-year period. Our targeted users include Web analysts, marketers and advertisers, and Web masters and administrators, who have a need to reduce the cost of accessing millions of pieces of related Web CUT information. The reduction in their cost of comprehending this immense amount of dynamic Web data enables sensemaking tasks to be done orders of magnitude faster than previous applications. Since Web sites and its associated usage data change daily, this cost-structure reduction is critical in maintaining timely Web sites.

2. Real-World Analysis Scenarios

We motivated the need of site administrators, content providers, and vusers to be able to perform exploratory sensemaking of Web sites. In this section, we show how the Web Analysis Visualization Spreadsheet (WAVS) is able to engage the user in a visual sensemaking cycle, and successively gather higher levels of information. Given the ability to operate on Web site analysis data, we can permute different operators to graphically process the data by supporting a visual sensemaking cycle.

Faddishness of Information. In our previous work [28, 79], we showed the importance of finding various patterns of faddishness in information. A problem encountered in using the Time Tubes visualization [28] is the choice of color scale for mapping frequency of usage. Each color scale has advantage and disadvantages. As a result, we typically found ourselves experimenting with many different color scales without finding a perfect scale. The Visualization Spreadsheet provided the appropriate tools for experimenting with this problem. By simply applying a change of the color scale across an entire row or column, we can simultaneously view the effect of frequency of usage in different contexts. The principle of *applying operators in parallel* enables this interaction with ease.

First Sensemaking Cycle: Cone Tree. In the vertical dimension of Figure 6.1, we choose to threshold the color scale so that it maps values between 0 and 100 in Row 1, and [100, 500] in Row 2, and [500, 2000] in Row 3. In the horizontal dimension, across the columns, we show the 1st, 2nd, 3rd, and 4th week of April 1997. The 5th column is the 3rd week in August 1997. We use Cone Trees to show the hierarchy, and the color scale is a rainbow heat scale where red correspond to high levels of usage, and blue correspond to low levels of usage. Here we are using the *value to structure mapping* principle to correlate between color scale and time. Figure 6.2 shows two particular features that emerged in Row 3 (color scale = [500,2000]). The feature marked by a yellow square corresponds to the sub-tree rooted at http://www.xerox.com/investor/content.html, while the feature marked by the yellow circle correspond to news.html. Both features show that the information rose in usage from the 1st week to the 3rd week and then lowered again on the 4th week. It is important to note that this feature is not visible in either Row 1 or 2.

Second Cycle: Disk Tree. After doing the interpretation step of the sensemaking cycle, we decided to try a different visual mapping transformation—Disk Tree [28]. Figure 6.3 shows the same data using Disk Trees instead of Cone Trees. Notice that while these two features are also visible on the third row, they were harder for the eye to pick up because the Disk Tree layout algorithm does not exaggerate the first several levels of the tree, while the Cone Tree layout algorithm does exaggerate the first few levels. On the other hand, it is much easier to comprehend the overall structure and usage pattern using the Disk Tree, because Disk Tree is a 2D technique that does not have occlusion problems. This example shows that different visualization techniques can contribute different senses in the sensemaking process. Here with the Disk Trees, we still use the *value to structure mapping* principle to correlate the color scales and time. We also used the *create analysis template* principle by reusing most of the spreadsheet format from the first cycle.

Correct Creation of New Content. Continuing with our case study, we wanted to find out the reason for the usage increase of these two areas of the Web site. By looking at the details around the area and examining the content, we found that on April 15, 1997, Xerox announced "New Digital Product Family Unveiled: Becomes Basis of Xerox Office Products into the Next Century"

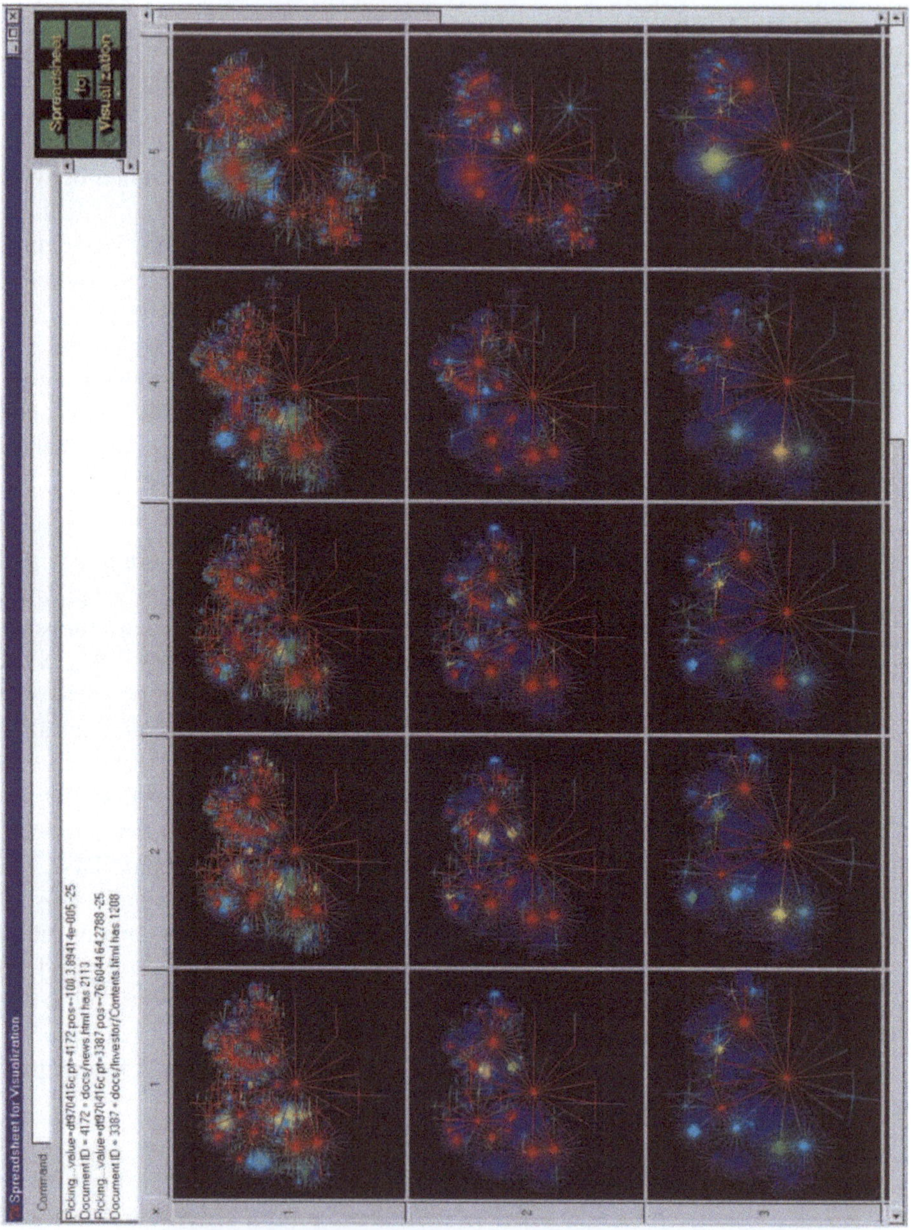

Figure 6.1. Web Analysis Visualization Spreadsheet showing the Xerox.com Web site using Cone Trees. Across the columns, we show the 1st, 2nd, 3rd, and 4th week of April 1997. The 5th column is the 3rd week in August 1997. We use Cone Trees to show the hierarchy, and the color scale is a rainbow heat scale where red correspond to high levels of usage, and blue correspond to low levels of usage. We choose to threshold the color scale so that it maps values between 0 and 100 in Row 1, and [100,500] in Row 2, and [500,2000] in Row 3.

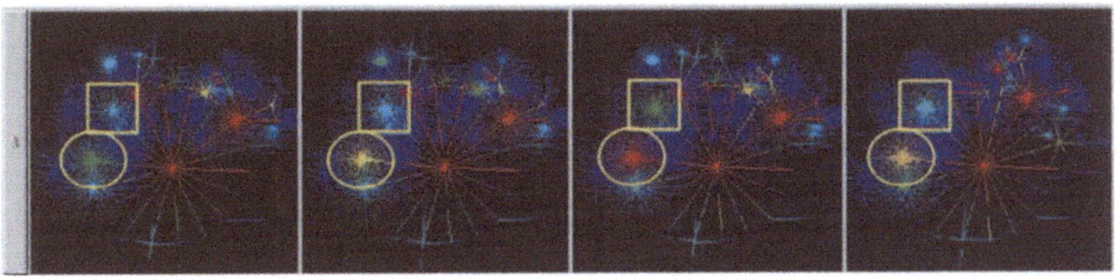

Figure 6.2. Faddish of Information in the Xerox.com Web site. The area marked by yellow first increases in usage, then decreases in the 4th week.

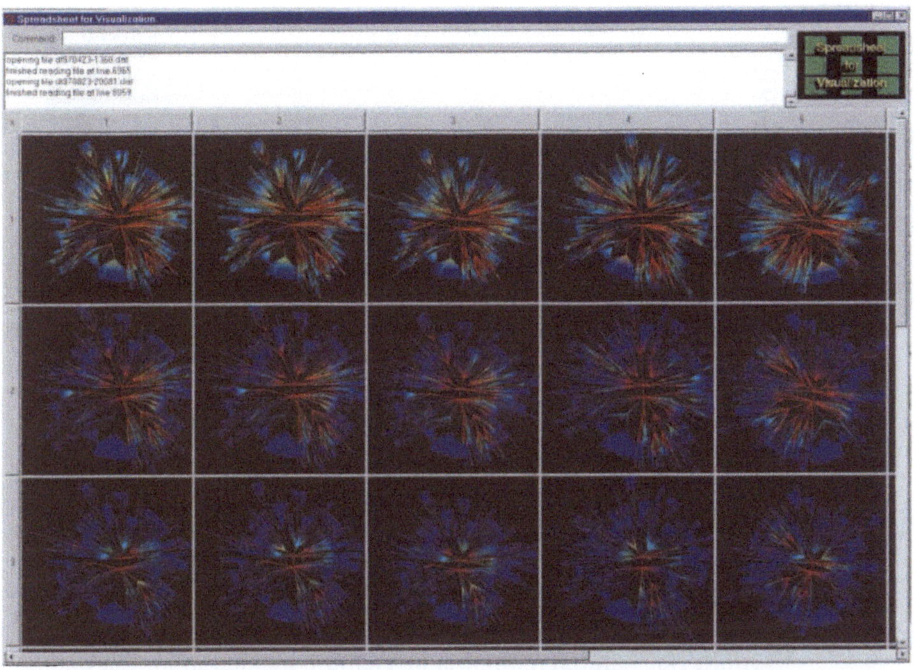

Figure 6.3. Web Analysis Visualization Spreadsheet with Disk Trees. While the faddish of information is visible, they are harder for the eye to pick up.

(http://www.xerox.com/PR/NR970415-newfam.html). A new product series was to present a new approach to network printing, faxing and scanning. In this press release, Xerox introduced two of its first products in this series, the Document Centre 220 and 230 Digital Copier. In looking into this press release, we found a new page linked off of the root node of the Web site that was the primary product page for this product series (/Products/XDC /content.html). The details of this area are shown in Figure 6.4. While it is immediately obvious that the pattern of usage as well as structure has changed on the 4th week, other less obvious visual features are also noticeable after careful examination. The feature marked by a long rectangle corresponds to this new product page, and its related pages. The red coloring of this entire area shows its high usage. Because this area is new and is being used extensively, this means the area shows a correct creation of new content that is highly desirable to Web users. The importance of the content is validated by the amount of attention it received.

Figure 6.4. Creation of new Web content for Product Families in Xerox.com. Parallel application of navigation operations enables examination of area details in different slices of the Disk Trees at the same time.

One lesson learned from this example is the usefulness of the *parallel application of operators*. By first selecting all of the cells in the first row, the user can simultaneously zoom, rotate, and translate to the same area of all of the Disk Trees. The spreadsheet affords this parallel operation in a natural manner, thus making the interaction easy and fast. In terms of the visual sensemaking cycle, it is imperative that we provide fast and easy interactions. By reducing the cost of interaction, we reduce the users' cognitive load for view manipulation so that they can concentrate on the task at hand, rather than minute details of the interface.

The other lesson we learned from this example is the importance of allowing quick access to detailed information. The detail-on-demand tool provides this via picking, and the amount of detail displayed is programmable via the spreadsheet's interpretive command line.

Surprising Increases or Decreases in Usage. Our interpretation of the visualizations has uncovered an interesting story around the introduction of an important product, and how it has affected the usage of the Web site. We are further interested in mining for changes in usage, no matter how small the changes may be. In order to accomplish this task, we realized that a new analytical abstraction must be computed—the subtraction of one usage pattern from another usage pattern.

Third Cycle: Visual Usage Pattern Subtraction. Figure 6.5 shows the result of constructing a new spreadsheet. Column one shows the result of subtracting week one from week two, while Column two is week three subtracted from week two, and Column three is week four subtracted from week three. In other words, we are showing the first order difference between the weekly usage patterns. In Row 1, we show only the negative values (blue on the color scale), and only the positive values (red) in Row 2. Row 3 shows both negative and positive values at the same time. The visual usage subtraction shows the rise of information for the Pagis^{TM} and TextBridge^{TM} home pages (marked with a yellow oval in Figure 6.5). On the other hand, the Copier's home page had increasing usage (marked with a yellow rectangle) only during the second week, but not the third or fourth week. Without the visual subtraction, these trends are not at all noticeable (see the straight usage-to-color mappings in Figure 6.6). Here we used the principle of *derive comparison data sets* to enable users to extract potentially interesting differences in the data.

Validation of Web Site Design.

Fourth Cycle: Relevance by Spreading Activation. As the last step in the visual sensemaking cycle, we wish to validate the Web site design using spreading activation. Using document similarity as our metric, we perform spreading activation over the web site. Figure 6.7 shows the result of performing this operation over the week of May 10, 1998. From left to right, we show the Web site in two day intervals. In the first Disk Tree, we spread over the supplies.html page, and the red vector glyphs show that move relevant documents are within its own sub-tree (marked in yellow). In the middle Disk Tree, however, the visualization shows that there are two clusters of documents in different parts of the hierarchy that have relevance to the workgroup.html node. The third Disk

Figure 6.5. Visual usage pattern subtraction shows differences in usage quickly. Column 1 = week 2 - week 1, Column 2 = week 3 - week 2, Column 3 = week 4 - week 3. Row 1 shows only negative values (blue), while Row 2 shows only positive values (red). Row 3 shows both negative and positive values at the same time.

Tree shows the relevant documents to the services.html node are in only one cluster. This example shows the documents in these parts of the Web are placed in relatively accessible positions ac-

Figure 6.6. Without the visual subtraction, straight usage-to-color mapping of usage pattern does not show difference in usage at all.

Figure 6.7. Spreading Activation visualization enable visualization of related contents using document similarity. The clusters are localized to sub-trees, which means the Web site is well-designed relative to these areas.

cording to document similarity. Here we use the principle of *applying operators in parallel*, because we apply the spreading activation mathematical analysis operator across the rows in parallel.

3. Summary

In this Chapter, we presented a case study of how to use the Visualization Spreadsheet in a specific analysis domain. We are interested in a series of techniques for Web Ecology and Evolution Visualization (WEEV). We constructed a Visualization Spreadsheet that support Web usage analysis.

We showed how the spreadsheet system supports a visual sense-making cycle by presenting real-world scenarios in the context of analyzing the entire Xerox Web site. We picked out visual cues that show patterns and trends in the relationships among content, usage and topology over time. By identifying and applying the visualization operators in Web ecology analysis, we have opened the door to the answers of many interesting Web site design questions. The Visualization Spreadsheet became a Web analysis workbench that provides users with a set of tools that can be combinatorically applied in various analysis tasks. As the case studies show, by using a spreadsheet we further expand the user's ability to interact with multiple data sets simultaneously.

Chapter 7

IMPLEMENTATION EXPERIENCE

Graphics is progressing even farther by giving a visible form to research and methodology.

—Jacques Bertin [15, p. 265]

The Visualization Spreadsheet was inspired by observing the success of a powerful concept—the spreadsheet. The invention of the VisiCalc numerical spreadsheet in 1979 enabled ordinary computer users to handle complex mathematical and statistical analysis and fueled the adoption of personal computers. Spreadsheets have proven to be highly successful tools for interacting with numerical data with numerous advantages. Users can easily organize large groups of numbers in cells arranged in tabular form, apply algebraic operations to cells, manipulating rows and columns of data simultaneously. Users can directly manipulate the numbers. Spreadsheets is useful as an end-user programming tool, especially in enabling user to define data dependencies and kept up-to-date automatically. These advantages enable users to explore "what-if" scenarios rapidly.

Extending from this concept, our novel idea is that, unlike traditional spreadsheets, each cell in a spreadsheet can hold an entire visualization of a large complex data set, its associated data selection criteria, and viewing specifications needed to create a full-fledged information visualization. Similarly, inter-cell operations become far more complex, stretching beyond simple arithmetic and string operations to encompass a range of domain-specific operators. The advantages of the spreadsheet metaphor translate easily into analogous tasks in visualization. The spreadsheet metaphor can be applied to a wide variety of user tasks where the primary data sets are represented in cells using visualization techniques. The Visualization Spreadsheet supports cells containing complex datasets, viewed through powerful visualizations, with constraints between cells linking both data and view attributes. Visualization Spreadsheet supports tasks that were difficult to accomplish previously.

In this Chapter, we document our experiences of building visualization systems based on the Data State Model, and in particular the Visualization Spreadsheet. Our experience is enhanced by collaborating with potential users in specific data domains. By documenting our experience, we hope that others can benefit from this implementation knowledge.

Our experiences with the spreadsheet paradigm consisted of two stages. In the first stage, we took a prototype-driven research approach in studying how spreadsheet environments can be employed for visualization. To this end, we constructed a prototype visualization spreadsheet system for molecular biology. We started with a complete visualization application that was built for studying genetic sequence similarity that has only a single visualization at a time on the screen, which we call a "single cell application". In the second stage, we used a visualization toolkit to build a general visualization spreadsheet called Spreadsheet for Information Visualization.

In this chapter, we first describe the system we built in the first prototype stage, then we describe our general visualization spreadsheet system.

1. Prototype: Spreadsheet for Similarity Reports

The first system is a domain-specific study on how spreadsheets can be structured and used in performing specific tasks in analyzing genetic sequence similarity reports, and is called "Spreadsheet for Similarity Reports" (SSR). The system is designed for biologists and their task of comparing similarity reports, which we presented in Chapter 5. The flexibility of the layout of a spreadsheet enables the user to compare the contents of a cell to other 3D representations of the same or related data in another cell.

SSR is built using the OpenGL graphics rendering library and the Motif X11 interface toolkit using the C++ programming language. SSR is a spreadsheet version of a non-spreadsheet system we call "AlignmentViewer" [31, 32]. It includes a computational steering environment for rapidly executing the similarity algorithm on multi-processor computers using different algorithm parameters. For analysis, it provides animation, filtering, and variable-to-axis mapping capabilities.

SSR uses noun-verb interaction techniques, to explore their suitability for spreadsheet-based information visualization. Each spreadsheet cell contains abstract data that is geometrically represented in 3D. The user first selects the cells (the noun), and then selects the operation to be performed on those cells (the verb). The user can specify in each cell how to map the higher dimensional data into 3D geometric representations. The user can construct other 3D geometric mappings of the same data, apply rotation, translation, and scaling/zooming to the cells, filter the data, or even animate the data over a variable in a cell.

The AlignmentViewer system was a single cell application that packaged many interactions that are necessary for the analysis task that the molecular biologists perform. Their need to compare and contrast several visualizations at the same time lead us to transform this single cell application into a spreadsheet system. We analyzed the task structure of the comparison analysis, and determined that the current single cell application model does not fulfill the need to support these tasks. Our experience of moving this application to the spreadsheet model is that the underlying rendering routines and program data structures had to be reimplemented. This is because a single cell application typically has its rendering routines hardwired into a single graphic context. This is true when using most graphic rendering libraries, including OpenGL. The conversion process was neither trivial nor easy. However, as shown in Chapter 5, the resulting system indeed supported the comparison task and provided the necessary interactions to the users.

Our experience with the first custom-tailored spreadsheet system proved that special purpose spreadsheets can be tailored to provide support for tasks that are difficult or impossible to perform with a single cell application. The question is whether a general purpose spreadsheet visualization system is feasible and useful.

2. Spreadsheet for Information Visualization Implementation

The second system is based on our prototype stage experience with SSR, and is a general visualization spreadsheet called "Spreadsheet for Information Visualization" (SIV, pronounced "sieve").

Figure 7.1, we show a diagram of the control flow of the system. The user interacts with the system via input devices, such as a mouse and keyboard. A command parser then decodes the input and feeds the result into a command interpreter. The executor is responsible for making sure that the commands are executed according to the instruction of the command interpreter.

To carry out the instructions, the executor modifies the memory, which consists of three parts: grid memory, dependency information, and command workspace. The grid memory holds the cells of a spreadsheet. A cell holds an entire raw data set. The dependency information specifies the relationships between the cells of the spreadsheet. A command workspace holds the temporary data that is generated during computation.

Graphical processing routines render the contents of the memory to the graphical display. When the user makes her input via the input device, she gets immediate feedback of her actions via a status field. Each cell view can occupy its own window for finer detail, and its dependency relationships are specified by commands in a formula entry box. The user gets her feedback via this graphical display to understand and make discoveries about the data sets in the cells.

Figure 7.2 shows the architecture of the SIV system. On top of the windowing system, we use a graphic rendering library, such as OpenGL. We use the C++ programming language. On top of C++, we use a visualization toolkit, which provides various visualization rendering techniques. We use a scripting language such as Tcl/Tk [76] to enable users and programmers to interact with the system using higher-level programming constructs than a complex lower-level language such as C++. We prepackage many often-used commands into procedures written in the scripting language. Finally, the user interacts with this entire system via a user interface, which is presented on the display to the user directly.

The system is built using the Visualization Toolkit (VTK) [91, 92]. We chose VTK because it provides an object-oriented architecture with many pre-built objects that we can use for exploring the spreadsheet paradigm. This is one of many advantages of us-

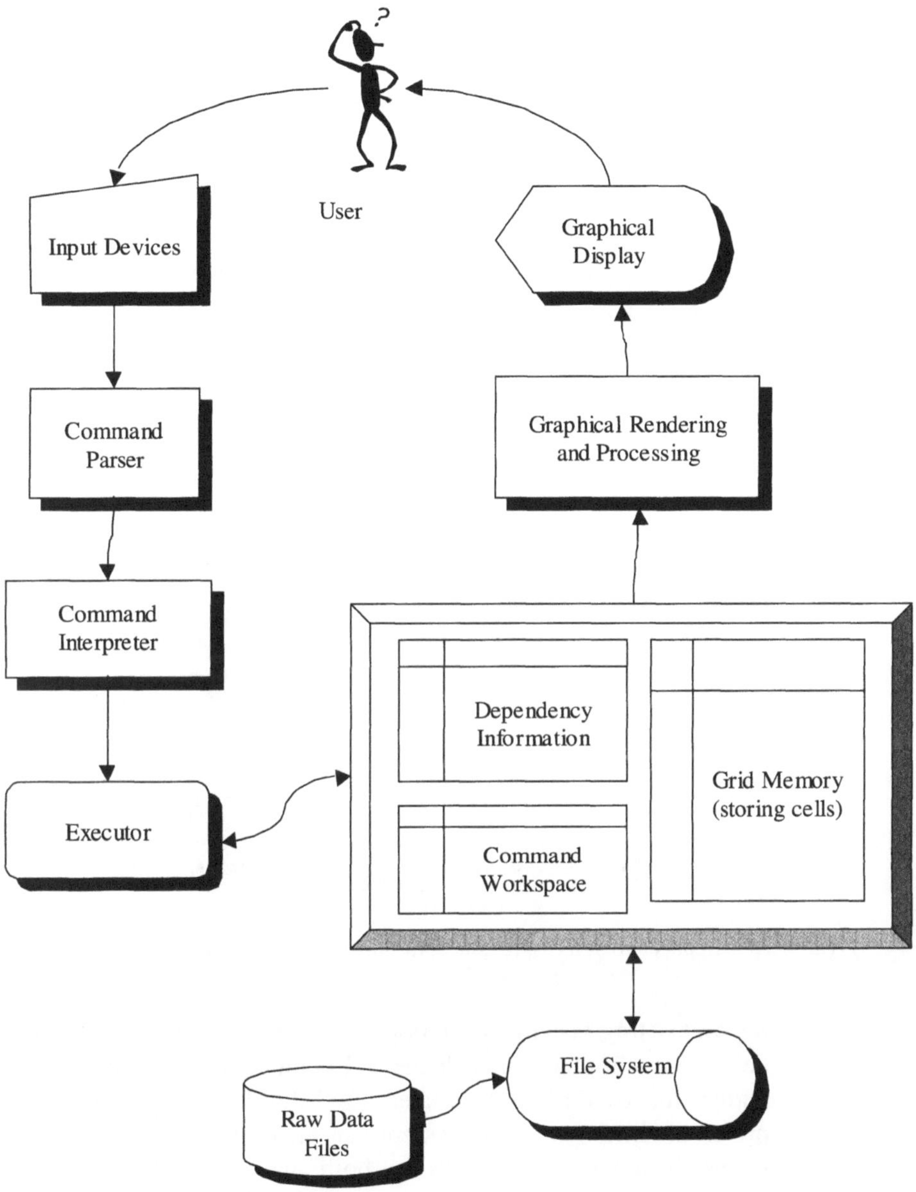

Figure 7.1. Interactions and Control Flow of the Spreadsheet for Information Visualization System

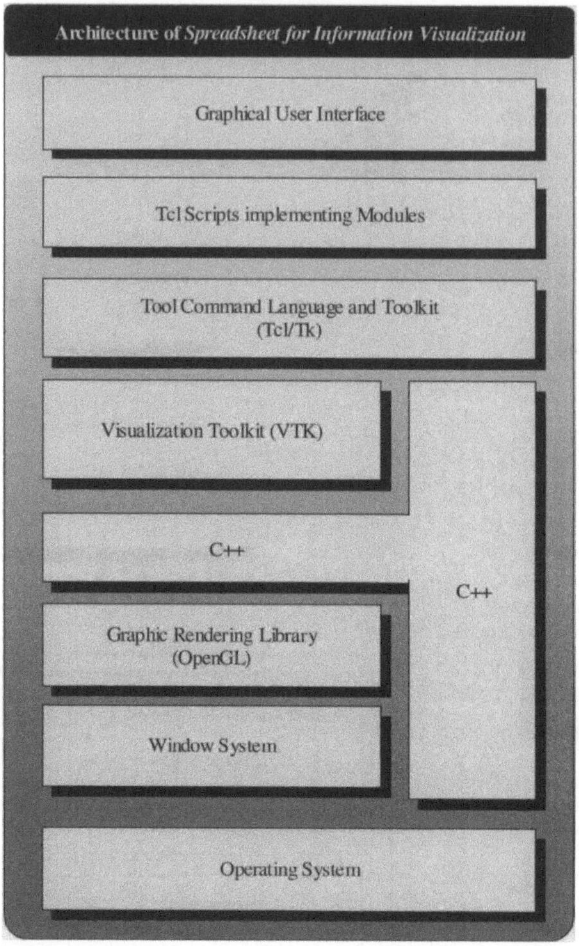

Figure 7.2. Architecture of the Spreadsheet for Information Visualization System

ing an existing visualization toolkit. For example, since VTK can be used in conjunction with the Tcl command language and Tk widget toolkit [76], it facilitates rapid development in an interpreted environment. The system can also run on multiple platforms since VTK and Tcl/Tk are both available under Unix and MS Windows. SIV is scalable and can handle any data sets that is importable into VTK. Given the standards of today's PCs, SIV can easily handle several cells of terrain data points of sixteen megabytes each, and other cells containing volume visualization of size 64 x 64 x 64 voxels or larger. For example, molecular biologists who were end-users in our initial design evaluation have used SIV on sequence similarity data sets as large as several hundred pages long. Our Web analysis examples in Chapter 5 contained linkage structures with 10,000-25,000 nodes.

3. Discussion

Task Tailored vs. General Purpose. The SSR prototype system is custom-tailored to the molecular biologists' task of comparing multiple sequence similarity reports. Its advantage is that since we know the data domain extremely well, due to our long-time collaboration with them, operations that are needed in their tasks are custom programmed and supported by drop-down menus. All operations were performed with a noun-verb interaction technique. This facilitates the ease-of-use of the system.

While the general purpose SIV system can be tailored to this task as well, it requires an application programmer to achieve the kind of user-friendliness that is available in the SSR system.

Scripting Language. The general purpose SIV system is customizable using the Tcl scripting language, which facilitates easy prototyping when we encounter a new visualization domain. It is fast to experiment with different visualization techniques that are already available in the visualization toolkit. If a new visualization technique is needed, it is often possible to construct new visualization operators directly using the scripting language and the visualization toolkit. The scripting language greatly enhanced the programmability of the spreadsheet system.

Visualization Toolkit. This programmability is enabled by the many pre-built visualization objects that were available in the VTK visualization toolkit [91, 92]. The techniques include graphic primitives (e. g. texture-mapping, lighting, surface rendering), scalar visualization, contouring, dividing cubes, marching cubes, vector visualization, glyphs, streamlines, streamtubes, tensor visualization, image processing, volume visualization, visualization modeling (e. g. decimation, implicit surfaces). The wide-variety of pre-built modules enabled fast and efficient prototyping that shift the spreadsheet programmer's attention away from "reinventing the wheel" and focuses it on the tasks at hand and the operators that are needed. The programmer can pay more attention to how operators fit in the Data State Model. In particular, these pre-built modules help programmers in creating the appropriate task-specific operators and in thinking about how these operators interface with the spreadsheet.

Operator Reuse. The advantage of using a scripting language and a visualization toolkit is that operators are not only easy to program, but they are also easy to reuse. Since most operators in the SIV system is implemented using scripts, the spreadsheet programmer can easily change the operators by modifying the scripts. Operators that are useful in one particular application domain often can be used unmodified or slightly modified in another application domain. For example, we have found the Disk Tree layout algorithm to be useful in visualizing many different hierarchical data in many different application domains. Once it is implemented in the Visualization Spreadsheet, it need not be re-implemented again.

As described in Chapter 2, operationally similar operators have very similar procedural patterns. So even in the case where these operators cannot be directly reused, we have found that we can often use the same procedural template.

Implementing Operators using Iterators. A design pattern that occurs often in the implementation of visualization operators is the need to iterate over a particular variable. The implementation of such operators can be simplified by using an object-oriented technique called "iterators", which is an object that provides access and traversal interfaces to a collection of objects. Many spreadsheet-level operators could even be described using iterators. For instance, copying an entire row or column simply requires an single iteration over the range of cells.

Using iterators to implement operators is a powerful technique. For example, for data sets that are represented using linked lists, addition can be performed by using two iterators that iterate over the two lists to merge them. Subtraction can be performed by iterating over one list while looking for the existence of the element in the other list.

Let us also describe how we can implement animation using iterators. Many application domains contain variables of nominal, ordinal, or quantitative types [24]. An iterator can be used to generate sequences of ordered sets of values from ordinal and quantitative types. We can then use these iterators to specify animations. So for variables that we already know the order, we can simply provide a default animation iterator. If a variable is nominal, we can still perform the same action by asking the user to specify an order between the named values. This is valid, because often the order of named values does not matter in the particular application domain.

Interestingly, by parameterizing the iterator, we can even get different step sizes. An iterator can even be applied over an variable that is not currently mapped onto the display [32]. For instance, we can dynamically query over the sales price of homes even if that variable is not shown on one of the axes.

The advantage of using iterators to implement operators is that we can build iterators without tying them to the underlying data type. The implementation of the operators then becomes independent of the data type and the data structure. This enables iterator reuse, and hence operator reuse. Operator reuse cuts programmers' costs by enabling rapid implementation.

4. Lessons Learned: Answers to High-Level Challenges

We now have evidences of our success. Over the past several years we have learned that the spreadsheet approach is a powerful and intuitive technique for interacting with information visualizations. Here we answer the High-Level Challenges from Section 1, which are the questions that we must answer to address the success of the project.

The first question is, "**How is the visualization spreadsheet valuable for user tasks and visualization applications?**"

The visualization spreadsheet idea is valuable in many visualization tasks. Information visualization systems confront such questions as how to represent abstract data visually, what types of exploratory interaction to include, and how to structure this interaction. Therefore, certain capabilities are critical, such as exploring different views of the data interactively, applying operations like rotation or data filtering to a view or group of views, and comparing two or more related datasets. The need to explore multiple visual representations simultaneously arises especially in information visualization. For example, in the time-series matrix visualization, different visualization techniques extract different visual features that represent distinct data patterns. The Visualization Spreadsheet is an excellent way to address these issues that involve multiple data sets and visualizations. These operations are natural in a spreadsheet environment.

The value of a visualization spreadsheet lies in enabling users to build multiple visual representations of data sets, perform operations on the visual representations, and compare and contrast the results visually. In the 3D Delaunay algorithm visualization example, algebraic operations made comparing different steps of the algorithm easier, because the user can see the operands and the results simultaneously. The spreadsheet paradigm is helpful in structuring certain interactions, such as cases where one change needs to be applied or propagated to other datasets. In the biological sequence similarity visualization, the parallel application of the rotation operator across an entire row of data sets enabled users to view the similarities between data sets in the same orientation. Because the spreadsheet provides a structured environment to perform tasks, it significantly reduce the amount of time it takes to analyze data.

The second question is, "**What kinds of user tasks are supported by the Visualization Spreadsheet environment?**" Alternatively, we could also ask, "**What properties of tasks make them suitable for spreadsheet-based interaction?**"

There are a large number of tasks that are particularly suitable. Here are some intuitive ones:

1 Tasks that explore "what-if" scenarios. For example, what if a different color scale is used? Or what if we look at the usage pattern of a Web site using different time ranges?

2 Tasks that involve exploring similar features of different data sets. For example, we can look at similar usage patterns from different time periods).

3 Tasks that study the interaction between two different variables. For example, we can look at the interaction between color scales and different time intervals in the Web analysis example.

4 Tasks that involve applying a single operation to multiple visualizations, such as applying similar selection, filtering, and highlighting to different data sets. For example, we can select an entire row of biological sequence similarity visualizations and rotate them coordinately.

Finally, the third question is, "**How general is the Visualization Spreadsheet paradigm?**"

The idea is general. The visualization spreadsheet paradigm is applicable to all visualization domains except a few situations. Sometimes a single-view application is sufficient for the task. Often a data-flow visualization system is more appropriate, because the focus is on how to translate the raw data into a visualization. The visualization spreadsheet paradigm supports a variety of tasks in situations involving multiple data sets or visualization techniques, parallel application of operations to multiple visualizations, derivation of comparison data sets, re-computation of dependencies between data sets, re-application of analysis templates, etc. The advantages of the Visualization Spreadsheet in these situations are evident in a variety of data domains. The thesis selected a variety of different types of data from several scientific disciplines and information fields: genetic sequence similarity from molecular biology, time-series matrices, algorithm visualization, and statistical data set patterns from a World-Wide Web site's content, usage, and structure.

The visualization spreadsheet principles discussed apply across a wide range of visualization applications, helping spreadsheet users understand how to take advantage of the power of the paradigm, and assisting developers understand how to structure their tools. In various example domains, the visualization spreadsheet principles arose while users applied operations to the data. In particular, in the visual sensemaking task of a large Web site, the visualization spreadsheet principles applied directly to help users extract data patterns.

5. Summary

We have developed a system that supports visualizations using a spreadsheet metaphor. The system supports the Data State Model we described in Chapter 2, and the many levels of visualization abstraction described in that model. We described the architecture of our general purpose Spreadsheet for Information Visualization system. As Chapter 5 has shown, the implementations we described in this chapter are successful in fulfilling many of the task scenarios that users encounter while they are trying to make sense of their large data sets.

Chapter 8

RELATED WORK

To construct a useful graphic, we must know what has come before and what is going to follow.

—Jacques Bertin [15, p. 16]

In this chapter, we present work related to the concepts of visualization reference models and visualization spreadsheets. We also peripherally mention visualization systems in general.

1. Reference Model for Information Visualization

Visualization can be viewed as a transformation process that converts data values into graphical views. In scientific visualization, many researchers and practitioners have examined the use of a data flow network for constructing visualizations [103, 43, 54]. For example, Schroeder et. al. [92] described a conceptual data flow model in the context of scientific visualization for applying operations to generate a visualization. The model consists of a visualization network that can contain multiple sources and sinks. Every step in the middle of the network consists of filters that have inputs and outputs.

The traditional data flow model used in scientific visualization is insufficient for describing information visualizations. This is because information visualizations often have a different set of requirements from scientific visualizations. Information visualization systems confront such questions as how to represent abstract data visually, what types of exploratory interaction to include, and how to structure this interaction. Because information visualization deals with abstract data that do not have inherent spatial mappings, the relationship between the value and the view becomes much more complex. Therefore, certain capabilities are critical, such as exploring different views of the data interactively, applying operations like rotation or data filtering to a view or group of views, and comparing two or more related datasets.

Some information visualizers have observed the intricate relationship between the view and the value associated with that view. One early observation was made by Becker in [10] that when using an interactive brushing[1] technique with a group of scatterplots, the effect of an operation on a data point appears simultaneously on all scatter plots in the other views. They termed this a "coordinated" interaction. There is only one data set, but many different views. This is a simple, yet-powerful, notion of view and value, where the views are always tied to the underlying value. This binding is never broken. The advantage of coordinated interactions is that the user has a very concise and clear model of how the system works. The disadvantage is that the opposing intention is impossible, which is that the user may just want to temporarily change one view, but not all of them. For example, the user may simply want to select a group of data points in one particular view to highlight it to discuss it outside the context of other scatter plots.

Later works explored the view/value relationship further by examining how view is dependent on the value. For example, Lee and Grinstein [60] presented a conceptual model for database visual exploration, which describes the analysis process as a series of value-to-value, value-to-view, view-to-value, and view-to-view transformations. They also describe the concept of generating metadata using database queries to aid in this process.

Chuah and Roth [33] extended Foley et. al.'s user interaction framework [38] by incorporating BVI (Basic Visualization Interactions), which is a more detailed characterization of data filters in the context of information visualization. They also presented a basic classification taxonomy for BVIs (shown in Figure 8.1).

Tweedie [102] presented a data transformation model similar to [60], an interactivity model that classifies the interactions based on the amount of control the user has over the process, and a state model similar to [33].

[1] In information visualization, brushing is a term used to describe a moving cursor that interactively specifies the area of focus for the current user interaction.

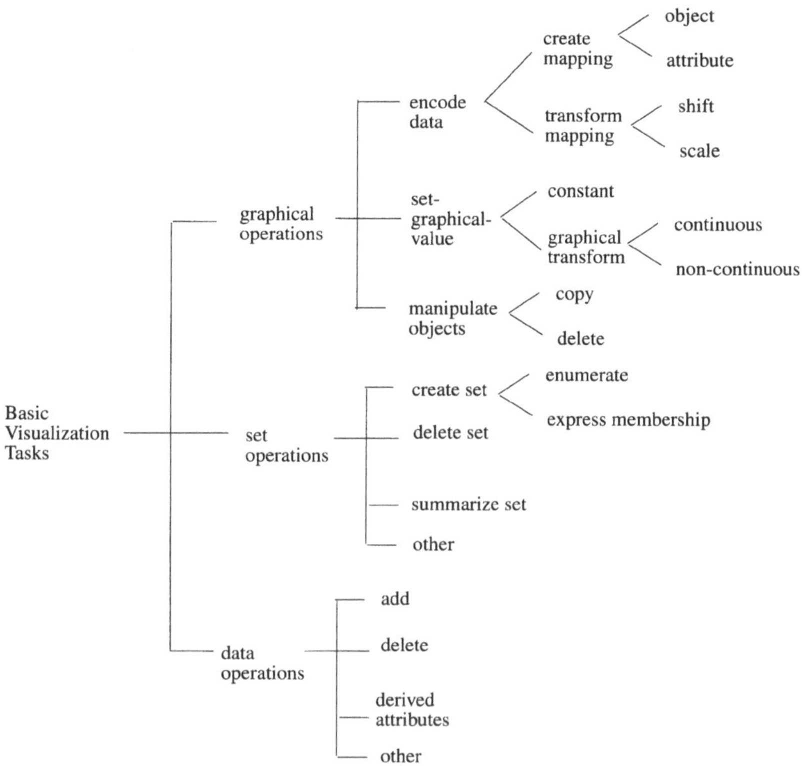

Figure 8.1. Chuah and Roth's Basic Visualization Interaction taxonomy

As we developed the Visualization Spreadsheet [30], we found that past models were not sufficiently detailed for describing operators and interactions in the Visualization Spreadsheet. We could not use Becker's "coordinated" method in [10], because the tight coupling of view/value completely disallows the view to operate independently of the value underneath, and we need this capability in the Visualization Spreadsheet. Lee and Grinstein [60] describes mostly database interactions, and their model is not general enough for detailed visualization interactions.

We were motivated by Chuah's BVI framework [33], and explored to what extent this taxonomy suits our needs. While the BVI model tied the interaction model with a state model, the state model lacks detail to help capture domain-specific designs. For example, it does not appear to handle operations with multiple semantics. The filter example at the beginning of Chapter 2 suggests that we could interpret dynamic query filters as either a value operation or a view operation. Under the BVI architecture, dynamic querying is classified as a graphical operation, which does not affect the underlying data. Moreover, we discovered that the relationship between "set operations" and "data operations" was unclear, and the semantics of view/value filtering ("shift" as defined in Figure 8.1) is confusing in this model. The "graphical operations" subtree is more detailed than other areas of the tree, which are less developed. The class of visual mapping operators needs more examination.

In Tweedie's framework, the data transformation model and the state model in her work are at the high level of abstraction. Because of the high level of abstraction, her model does not deal with domain-specific interactions in a detailed way. For example, her model could not be used to evaluate information visualization systems that have multiple data sources and views.

Most importantly, past models also failed to unify the interaction model with the visualization process. For example, the visualization pipeline as described by Stuart Card [24] is a rich design space that has yet to be unified with a complete interaction model. As another example, Chuah and Roth's work, which unified the low-level keyboard/mouse interactions, did not incorporate this visualization pipeline.

We need a model that describes how the graphical, data, and control states are affected by the operators. Here we are trying to extend past work by unifying a taxonomy of operators with the visualization pipeline that uniquely solves the above problems.

2. Spreadsheet

Spreadsheets are one of the few true success stories among systems for end-user programming—that is, systems designed to allow non-programming users to create computations of their own design. —Scott Hudson [48]

People have long used tables to organize information. More recently, the invention of the VisiCalc numerical spreadsheet in 1979 fueled the adoption of personal computers [21]. The spreadsheet naturally extends the tabular organization of information by allowing the user to specify and interact with the contents and the interconnections of the cells. The spreadsheet paradigm has been suggested in earlier work for domains such as images, volume visualization, and financial data. Here we review the literature related to spreadsheet-based visualization systems.

Tabular Organizations. Mathematicians and statisticians use tables of sine, cosine, and confidence probabilities. Statisticians have examined visualizing higher dimensional point sets by a table of projections. For example, one multivariate analysis tool is the scatter matrix, which is a table of scatter plots (see [34]). Visualization researchers have applied similar ideas, but in different ways, to produce a table of views of a single dataset [105, 6]. In the scatter matrix, a statistics researcher may mark a datum in one scatter plot, and the program would then highlight the corresponding point in all other scatter plots. These approaches represent a largely static tabular approach to the data, but some interactivity is present, such as rotations, translation, and zooming.

Spreadsheets for Visual Programming. Spenke and Beilken's PREPLEX system uses constraints and a spreadsheet interface for logic programming [94]. Spreadsheet cells on fixed grids are Prolog variables and constrained using Prolog predicates. PREPLEX is based on earlier suggestions in the logic programming community [96, 104, 58].

There are many visual programming data-flow language systems, such as Forms/3 [108, 45] and Fabrick [52]. Forms/3, implemented using the Garnet constraint system [70], uses cells that are free-floating and attached to graphical objects such as line boxes and buttons. Textual formulas or programming statements can then be entered as cell values in a dialog box. Even though it has been called a "spreadsheet", its similarity to spreadsheets is limited to data propagation and textual formulas, and therefore is more accurately termed "form-based" [45, page 4].

Spreadsheets for User Interface Design. Two notable systems designed for user interface specification are the Penguims system [49, 48], and the C32 spreadsheet [69] in the Garnet toolkit [70]. The purpose of both systems is to enable user interface programmers to specify complex constraints among user interface elements by using equations in cells. The Penguims system does not strictly conform to a grid, but instead organizes cells into related stacks. In both systems, the spreadsheet is used to specify the user interface, but not to display the result, which appears in a separate window.

Related User Interface Techniques. There are several distortion presentation techniques based on a tabular layout [62] such as Document Lens [86], fish-eye views [39, 89], stretching rubber sheets [90]. Many of these techniques have been applied directly to a tabular organization to provide global context viewing and detailed focused zooming, e.g. Table Lens [83]. As another example, DataSpace [6] used 3D lattices and cone trees to lay out images in 3D space.

In addition, MagicLenses and see-through tools [97, 16, 17] are relevant, since they can provide zooming and other interactive filtering capabilities. For example, a debugging lens may be placed over the spreadsheet to reveal dependencies between cells. Other examples of relevant user interface techniques include Pad++ [12, 11], which can be used to organize several spreadsheets at different depths.

Spreadsheets are also related to the area of constraint languages and systems [70, 20, 19, 18, 73, 112]. Constraints are relationships that are declared once and then maintained by the system. Constraints are relevant to spreadsheets since values of cells are constrained by equations. Spreadsheets use single-direction data propagation, thus can be viewed as *one-way constraint* systems. Although not in common use, spreadsheets can be built using *inxmulti-way constraints*, where data propagation occurs in both directions [96].

Spreadsheets for Images. Past spreadsheet work has focused mostly on data that can readily be visualized with a straight mapping, e.g. numbers, or images. The first spreadsheet that allows the display of images in a cell is ASP [77], but it contains no advanced capabilities. The "Spreadsheets for Images" (SI) system [63] and the Interactive Image Spreadsheet (IISS) system [44] examine ways to profitably extend the spreadsheet paradigm to images. For example, in [63] Levoy shows how a spreadsheet can be used to examine an image processing pipeline, and in [44] Hasler shows how many image processing tasks can be efficiently organized in a spreadsheet system. "Spreadsheet for Images" [63] mentions the importance of data flow in spreadsheet. Levoy also briefly mentions volume visualization in the context of his tool. Most of the interactions in his tool are implemented as Tcl [76] commands, with certain geometric operations implemented using direct manipulation. These two systems illustrate some of the capabilities made possible by extending the spreadsheet paradigm to other domains.

Data Flow Visualization Systems. Interest in visualization-based user interfaces has blossomed in the past few years, with systems developed for application areas from hypertext information to geology, molecular biology, file system structure, and animal behavior patterns. Large visualization systems contain modules that users can hook together into a data-flow network to create visualizations. These systems offer many advantages for rapidly building applications. The success of these systems attests to the utility of modular, easy-to-use, extensible tools for visualization tasks. Examples of such systems include ConMan [43], AVS [103, 8], IRIS Explorer [54], IBM Data Explorer [50, 1], and Visualization Toolkit (VTK) [91, 92]. In general, existing visualization systems are designed for visualizing a single dataset at a time.

Visual Interactive Spreadsheets. Past work in the visualization community has produced interactive tables for specific applications, and include systems such as TableLens [83], FOCUS [95], a graphical financial spreadsheet called FINESSE [106]. The TableLens system [83], designed for browsing tabular numerical information, looks much like a conventional spreadsheet with bar graphs. The FOCUS interactive table, modeled after TableLens, allows sophisticated navigation via sorting and hiding of information contained in the table, but lacks editing capabilities [95]. FOCUS is similar to TableLens, with the main difference between the two in the interaction methods. TableLens uses a fish-eye layout strategy for display, whereas FOCUS uses a dynamic querying mechanism as the primary interaction method. FINESSE is a prototype system designed for financial data, where the cells are on fixed grids and contain four representation primitives—line plots, 3D surface plots, heat maps, or 3D bar graphs.

The NoPumpG prototype [109] system abandons the fixed tabular grid of conventional spreadsheets, so all cells are free floating. It allows the specification of line plots based on sliders attached to variable values [109]. It is compared to a spreadsheet because of its data dependency capabilities.

Most recently, after our work, Jankun-Kelly and Ma described their work on a visualization spreadsheet interface [55], further suggesting the power of the spreadsheet metaphor as applied to information visualization.

Analysis of Related Spreadsheet Research. The Visualization Spreadsheet is a natural extension of the above ideas. Our work focuses on the area of information visualization, and the issues that arise prominently in that domain. We build upon the experiences of other spreadsheets mentioned above, and include a variety of different visual representations and operations useful for interacting with the visualizations.

We build upon the experience of numeric spreadsheets. We explicitly keep the numeric spreadsheet features of tabular grid layout, operators that specify operations and relationships between cells, and automatic recomputation of dependent data sets. We apply these concepts to visualization so that each cell can contain an entire visualization, which includes the underlying abstract data sets, the sequence of data transformations and the associated viewing parameters.

The image spreadsheets (IISS and SI) focused on images, and the associated image operations. Images, however, are a straight forward mapping from value to view. In a sense, the view is the value, and there is very little discernible differences between the two. Therefore, the operator model for an image spreadsheet is limited to only image processing operations in comparison to a full-blown visualization system. We take a similar approach to the SI system in using Tcl as the command language [76], but we focus on the tasks and operation associated with information visualization.

Our work is most like FINESSE [106], but differs from FINESSE because our system allows animation, dynamic visual filtering [32, 2], and dynamic mapping of variables to representation. FINESSE has a limited number of cell primitives, whereas our system allows a wide variety of geometric primitives, since our system is built on top of the Visualization Toolkit (VTK) [91, 92]. Using a command language, our system also allows users to construct their own visual representations of their data. FINESSE focuses on financial data, whereas our system can be tailored to any information visualization tasks.

Lastly, in contrast to the visualization spreadsheet, existing large visualization systems are designed for viewing a single visualization at a time. In contrast to spreadsheet systems, in data flow systems, a large amount of screen space is devoted to the operators, rather than the operands. We believe that for many applications spreadsheets can provide better interaction.

A number of researchers applied the spreadsheet concept selectively to a few data domains, mostly images, and mentioned its possible wide applicability to visualization tasks. Our review indicates that work is needed to define the visualization spreadsheet's advantages and uncover frameworks for implementing the spreadsheet concept. By examining the structure of sensemaking, we seek to show the inherent capacity of the spreadsheet metaphor for supporting user tasks.

3. Summary

Here we reviewed prior work related to information visualization reference models in general and in particular the applications of the spreadsheet concept to visualization-related areas.

Typically, information visualization is accomplished by carefully examining the task requirements and then designing an application that fits the needs of the user. However, not all needs can be anticipated ahead of time. The exploratory nature of many tasks suggests that we need to construct an environment that provides a set of data and graphic processing primitives that users can employ as needed. Two critical elements in creating this kind of system are: (a) the creation of a visualization model that tracks the data states and enables the modeling and viewing of intermediate results, and (b) a concrete user interface instantiation of this model, which we call the Visualization Spreadsheet, which is geared to achieve a version of this environment.

Chapter 9

CONCLUSION

Information is the reply to a question.

—Jacques Bertin [15, p. 11]

Since the mid-nineteenth century, the use of statistical graphics to explain numbers has become a fixture in communicating information in our daily lives in newspapers and magazines. Since the early 1980s, we have seen an explosion of the use of scientific visualization in computational analysis of complex problems. Since the late 1980s, information visualization techniques have emerged to push the visualization frontier to abstract information that does not have an inherent spatial representation. Information is no longer simply passive graphics on paper. Visualization promises to change the way people interact with information by making information come alive on the computer screen.

Indeed, visualization research spans a remarkable range of scientific and non-scientific disciplines and corresponding visualization techniques. Visualization researchers have discovered that certain operations are needed across this entire range. These operations include comparing visualizations of two different datasets, as well as performing algebraic operations on two or more visualizations, such as visualizing the difference between two datasets. The challenge is to organize these complex visualization interactions into a coherent framework.

This need took us to develop the Visualization Spreadsheet. In developing the visualization spreadsheet paradigm, a visualization operator and interaction framework called the *Data State Model* arose. This model is general, as it is applicable to a variety of information visualization techniques. The model is as expressive as the Data Flow Model, but emphasizes the state of the data rather than the flow of the data. By modeling data set operations as data moves through the various stages of the visualization pipeline, the Data State Model categorizes operations into seven different basic types. The categorization of numerous information visualization techniques and its associated operations in Chapter 3 shows the generality of the Data State Model.

In this book, we have shed some light on the general utility of the visualization spreadsheet paradigm. First, the Visualization Spreadsheet is valuable in data analysis tasks, especially in information visualization, where users confront various ways of viewing and interacting with the data. The abstraction of visualization spreadsheet principles makes the value of the spreadsheet-based interaction especially clear. Second, gaining knowledge of the properties of suitable tasks for spreadsheet-based interaction enables researchers to identify future situations where the Visualization Spreadsheet is useful. Lastly, the Visualization Spreadsheet and the Data State Model are general frameworks that are applicable to a variety of data domains. In particular, the Data State Model enables researchers to taxonomize the space of visualization interactions. Undoubtedly, we will discover future benefits of the visualization spreadsheet paradigm.

To summarize, the contribution of this book include:

1 consolidating visualization interactions and operations under one operator framework called the Data State Model, by studying and building on current interaction models. We based our design of the model by collaborating with domain experts in several fields.

2 proving the visualization equivalence between the Data State Model and the Data Flow Model.

3 illustrating the usage of the Data State Model by characterizing and categorizing numerous visualization techniques and their associated operations.

4 providing a structured, intuitive, and powerful interface concept called the Visualization Spreadsheet, for investigating information visualizations of abstract multidimensional data sets.

5 specifying, constructing, and evaluating the Visualization Spreadsheet. In our research, we first carefully studied several existing and new applications

in several domains to identify requirements. We then used these requirements along with ideas from existing systems to design and implement a visualization spreadsheet framework. We evaluated this framework by using it in real-world scenarios.

6 confronting the challenge of visualizing a variety of different types of data, and illustrating the visualization spreadsheet principles in these various data domains. We showed the important capabilities offered by the Visualization Spreadsheet.

7 answering a set of key research questions and challenges on the effectiveness of the framework, and evaluating how the Visualization Spreadsheet concept meets the needs of users.

Visual information processing is not instantaneous, as there is no such thing as an automated analysis machine. However, visualization systems, such as our Visualization Spreadsheet, provide tools to reduce the cost-structure of obtaining information for the next step of the analysis. By carefully analyzing a particular domain (e.g. the Web site analysis task described in Chapter 5), the total time spent on a study can be significantly reduced.

A cognitive task structure called sensemaking has been developed to describe user interface tasks [88], which we mentioned in Chapter 1. Bertin mentions the five major stages of decision-making in [15]. In thinking about the visualization operator framework, we use these five major stages to define the finer grain Visual Sensemaking Cycle. Figure 9.1 shows the Visual Sensemaking Cycle and its various stages. The gray boxes denote Bertin's five stages of decision-making.

Here we show that the visualization operators defined in the model and implemented in our Visualization Spreadsheet system helps users carry out the various stages of the sensemaking cycle. We apply the sensemaking cycle to the Web site analysis task scenario.

1 Defining the problem: An analyst, when faced with a problem, first defines the problem by asking certain questions. Sometimes the questions are formed in the context of a hypothesis. For example, are certain areas of the Web site accessed more than other areas? Does the access pattern in these areas change over time?

2 Defining the data: Once the problem is framed in the context of hypotheses, the analyst must now gather the raw data that are necessary for analysis. In our example, the raw data would be the content of the Web site, the usage logs of the site, and the linkage structure or topology of the documents.

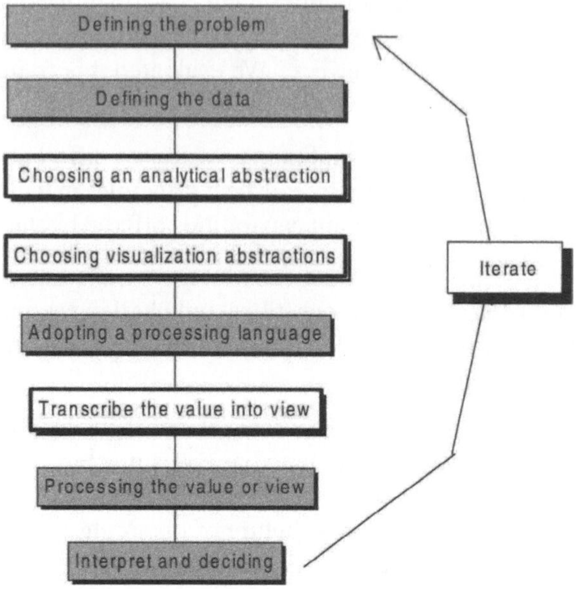

Figure 9.1. Stages of the Visual Sensemaking Cycle

3 Choosing an analytical abstraction: The raw data must be organized into data structures for easy access and query later. E.g. we extract the linkage information into a graph specified using adjacency lists.

4 Choosing various visualization abstractions: Visualization researchers know certain information abstractions are visualizable. Depending on the structure of the analytical abstractions and the visualization techniques that are available to the task, developers can choose among a variety of visualization abstractions, or new techniques must be invented to visualize new analytical abstractions. For example, visualization researchers know that visualizing a graph network of on the order of 100 nodes is difficult. Unfortunately, the graph of the Xerox Web site is on the order of 10,000 nodes. In the WAVS system, to solve this problem and in order to take advantage of the hierarchical nature of the Xerox Web site, we could choose a hierarchical representation for our visualization abstraction. We preserve back links as part of the detail-on-demand information.

5 Adopting a processing language: The next step in visual sensemaking is to determine the operators that are appropriate for the task. We have discussed at length the kind of operators that are needed in Web analysis in this chapter.

6 Transcribe the value into view: This stage is essentially the execution of the visualization pipeline to generate a new visualization state. The user sees visualizations that will try to shed light on the hypothesis that was posed earlier in stage 1.

7 Processing the value or view: At this stage, the analyst perform certain interactive operators on the results, such as rotation, scaling, detail-on-demand zooming, value-filtering.

8 Interpret and deciding: The analyst cognitively process the visualization in order to understand the features that are brought forth by these specific views.

9 Iterate: Specific features will grab our attention in the visualized results. Further hypotheses will be formed, and new visualizations will then need to be constructed to answer those questions. The process repeats until the analyst is satisfied that she has completely made sense of the data.

The power of visual sensemaking comes from the combinatorics of visualization operators. There exists a variety of ways in which the operators can be combined to answer new questions. This combination of operators covers a large conceptual space, where some of concepts are not even conceived ahead of time. By reducing the amount of time spent in between steps, "what-if" hypotheses and sensemaking cycles are accomplished in a matter of hours or minutes rather than days or weeks.

By describing how the Visualization Spreadsheet enables users to interact with and process visualizations, we showed its advantages in the analytical process of making sense of complex data sets, such as an evolving document collection as large as the entire Xerox Web site. By mapping data values to structures in the Visualization Spreadsheet, the user is engaged in a sensemaking cycle of mapping, perceiving, and cognitively processing informational graphics. Using a variety of visualization techniques, we showed that the interactions of the Visualization Spreadsheet help users draw conclusions from the overall relationships of the entire information set.

By enabling key analysis tasks, we have shown that the spreadsheet approach is a powerful and intuitive technique for interacting with the information visualizations in a structured way. It is conceivable that one day there will be a Visualization Spreadsheet available on every desktop computer just as most computers have numeric spreadsheets today.

The key to the success of information analysis is that the assembly of new visualizations must proceed at about the same rate as the analysis. By providing an operator framework that is concise and easy-to-understand, our Data State Model and the Visualization Spreadsheet framework achieve the goal of quickly adapting a tool to various analysis situations.

References

[1] Greg Abram and Lloyd Treinish. An extended data-flow architecture for data analysis and visualization. *Computer Graphics*, 29(3), May 1995.

[2] Christopher Ahlberg and Ben Shneiderman. Visual information seeking: Tight coupling of dynamic query filters with starfield displays. In *Proceedings of ACM CHI'94 Conference on Human Factors in Computing Systems*, volume 1, pages 313–317, 1994. Color plates on pages 479-480.

[3] Stephen Altschul, Warren Gish, Webb Miller, Eugene Myers, and David Lipman. Basic Local Alignment Search Tool. *Journal of Molecular Biology*, 215:403–410, 1990.

[4] J. R. Anderson and Peter L. Pirolli. Spread of activation. *Journal of Experimental Psychology: Learning, Memory, and Cognition*, 10:791–798, 1984.

[5] Keith Andrews. Visualizing cyberspace: Information visualization in the harmony internet browser. In *Proceedings of the Symposium on Information Visualization '95*. IEEE CS, 1995. Atlanta, Georgia.

[6] V. Anupam, S. Dar, T. Leibfried, and E. Petajan. DataSpace: 3-D visualizations of large databases. In *Proceedings of the Symposium on Information Visualization '95*, pages 82–88,144,145, 1995.

[7] Astra SiteManager. http://www.merc-int.com, 1997.

[8] Advanced Visualization System home page. http://www.avs.com, February 1999.

[9] R. A. Becker, S. G. Eick, and A. R. Wilks. Visualizing network data. *IEEE Transaction on Visualization and Computer Graphics*, 1(1):16–28, 1995.

[10] Ronald A. Becker and William S. Cleveland. Brushing scatterplots. *Technometrics*, 29(2):127–142, 1987.

[11] Benjamin B. Bederson and James D. Hollan. Pad++: A zooming graphical interface for exploring alternate interface physics. In *Proceedings of the ACM Symposium on User Interface Software and Technology*, pages 17–26, 1994.

[12] Benjamin B. Bederson, Larry Stead, and James D. Hollan. Pad++: Advances in multiscale interfaces. In *Proceedings of ACM CHI'94 Conference on Human Factors in Computing Systems*, volume 2, pages 315–316, 1994.

[13] Dennis Benson, Mark Boguski, David Lipman, and James Ostell. GenBank. *Nucleic Acids Research*, 22(17):3441–3444, 1994.

[14] Jacques Bertin. *Semiology of Graphics: Diagrams, Networks, Maps*. University of Wisconsin Press, Madison, WI, 1967/1983.

[15] Jacques Bertin. *Graphics and Graphic Information Processing*. Walter de Gruyter, 1981.

[16] Eric A. Bier, Maureen C. Stone, Ken Fishkin, William Buxton, and Thomas Baudel. A taxonomy of see-through tools. In *Proceedings of ACM CHI'94 Conference on Human Factors in Computing Systems*, volume 1, pages 358–364, 1994.

[17] Eric A. Bier, Maureen C. Stone, Ken Pier, William Buxton, and Tony DeRose. Toolglass and Magic Lenses: The see-through interface. In James T. Kajiya, editor, *Computer Graphics (SIGGRAPH '93 Proceedings)*, volume 27, pages 73–80, August 1993.

[18] A. Borning and R. Duisberg. Constraint-based tools for building user interfaces. *ACM Transactions on Graphics*, 5:345–374, October 1986.

[19] Alan Borning. Defining constraints graphically. In *Proceedings of ACM CHI'86 Conference on Human Factors in Computing Systems*, pages 137–143, 1986.

[20] Alan Borning. The progamming language aspects of ThingLab, a constraint-oriented simulation laboratory. *ACM Transactions on Programming Lanauges and Systems*, 3:353–387, October 1986.

[21] Polly S. Brown and John D. Gould. An experimental study of people creating spreadsheets. *ACM Transactions on Office Information Systems*, 5(3):258–272, July 1987.

[22] Vannevar Bush. As we may think. *Atlantic Monthly*, 176:101–108, 1945.

[23] Stuart Card, Steve Eick, and Nahum Gershon, editors. *Proceedings of the Symposium on Information Visualization '96*. IEEE CS, 1996. San Francisco, California.

[24] Stuart K. Card and Jock Mackinlay. The structure of the information visualization design space. In *Proceedings of the Symposium on Information Visualization '97*, pages 92–99. IEEE CS, 1997. Phoenix, Arizona.

[25] Stuart K. Card, Jock Mackinlay, and Ben Shneiderman. *Readings in Information Visualization: Using Vision to Think*. Morgan Kaufmann, 1999.

[26] Stuart K. Card, George G. Robertson, and William York. The WebBook and the Web Forager: An Information Workspace for the World-Wide Web. In *Proceedings of ACM CHI 96 Conference on Human Factors in Computing Systems*, volume 1, pages 111–117, 1996.

[27] Ed H. Chi. WebSpace Visualization. http://www.geom.umn.edu/docs/weboogl/ webspace/, 1994. The Geometry Center, University of Minnesota (Also appeared in First WWW Conference, Chicago, IL. November 1994).

[28] Ed H. Chi, James Pitkow, Jock Mackinlay, Peter Pirolli, Rich Gossweiler, and Stuart K. Card. Visualizing the evolution of web ecologies. In *Proceedings of ACM CHI 98 Conference on Human Factors in Computing Systems*, volume 1, pages 400–407, 1998. color plate on pp. 644-645.

[29] Ed H. Chi and John T. Riedl. An operator interaction framework for visualization systems. In *Proceedings of the Symposium on Information Visualization '98*, pages 63–70. IEEE CS, October 1998. Research Triangle Park, North Carolina.

[30] Ed Huai-hsin Chi, Phillip Barry, John Riedl, and Joseph Konstan. A spreadsheet approach to information visualization. In *Proceedings of the Symposium on Information Visualization '97*, pages 17–24,116. IEEE CS, 1997. Phoenix, Arizona.

[31] Ed Huai-hsin Chi, Phillip Barry, Elizabeth Shoop, John Carlis, Ernest Retzel, and John Riedl. Visualization of biological sequence similarity search results. In *Proc. IEEE Visualization '95*, pages 44–51. IEEE CS, 1995. Atlanta, Georgia.

[32] Ed Huai-hsin Chi, John Riedl, Elizabeth Shoop, John V. Carlis, Ernest Retzel, and Phillip Barry. Flexible information visualization of multivariate data from biological sequence similarity searches. In *Proc. IEEE Visualization '96*, pages 133–140, 477. IEEE CS, 1996. San Francisco, California.

[33] Mei C. Chuah and Steven F. Roth. On the semantics of interactive visualization. In *Proceedings of the Symposium on Information Visualization '96*, pages 29–36. IEEE CS, 1996. San Francisco, California.

[34] W.S. Cleveland and M.E. McGill, editors. *Dynamic Graphics for Statistics*. Wadsworth & Brooks/Cole, Belmont, CA, 1988.

[35] M. O. Dayhoff, R. M. Schwartz, and B. C. Orcutt. A model of evolutionary change in proteins. In M. O. Dayhoff, editor, *Atlas of Protein Sequence and Structure, Vol. 5, Suppl. 3*, chapter 22, pages 345–352. National Biomedical Research Foundation, 1978.

[36] John Dill and Nahum Gershon, editors. *Proceedings of the Symposium on Information Visualization '97*. IEEE CS, 1997. Phoenix, Arizona.

[37] S. Feiner and C. Beshers. Visualizing n-dimensional virtual worlds with n-vision. *Computer Graphics*, 24(2):37–38, 1990.

[38] James D. Foley, A. vanDam, S. K. Feiner, and J. F. Hughes. *Computer Graphics: Principles and Practice*. Addison-Wesley, 1990.

[39] George W. Furnas. Generalized fisheye views. In *Proceedings of ACM CHI'86 Conference on Human Factors in Computing Systems*, pages 16–23, 1986.

[40] Nahum Gershon and Steve Eick, editors. *Proceedings of the Symposium on Information Visualization '95*. IEEE CS, 1995. Atlanta, Georgia.

[41] Warren Gish and David States. Identification of protein coding regions by database similarity search. *Nature Genetics*, 3:266–272, 1993.

[42] Graph Visualizer 3D. http://www.omg.unb.ca/hci/projects/gv3d/, March 1998.

[43] Paul E. Haeberli. ConMan: A visual programming language for interactive graphics. In John Dill, editor, *Computer Graphics (SIGGRAPH '88 Proceedings)*, volume 22, pages 103–111, August 1988.

[44] A. F. Hasler, K. Palaniappan, and M. Manyin. A high performance interactive image spreadsheet (IISS). *Computers in Physics*, 8(3):325–342, May/June 1994.

[45] Judith G. Hays and Margaret M. Burnett. A guided tour of Forms/3. Technical Report TR 95-60-6, Oregon State University, Computer Science Department, June 1995. (Revised Janurary 1997).

[46] R. J. Hendley, N. S. Drew, A. M. Wood, and R. Beale. Narcissus: Visualizing information. In *Proceedings of the Symposium on Information Visualization '95*. IEEE CS, 1995. Atlanta, Georgia.

[47] Steven Henikoff and Jorga Henikoff. Performance evaluation of amino acid substitution matrices. *Proteins: Structure, Function, and Genetics*, 17:49–61, 1993.

[48] Scott E. Hudson. User interface specification using an enhanced spreadsheet model. *ACM Transactions on Graphics*, 13(3):209–239, July 1994.

[49] Scott E. Hudson and Shamim P. Mohamed. Interactive specification of flexible user interface displays. *ACM Transactions on Information Systems*, 8(3):269–288, 1990.

[50] IBM Visualization Data Explorer (DX). http://www.almaden.ibm.com/dx/, February 1999. (current as of date).

[51] Takeo Igarashi, Jock D. Mackinlay, Bay-Wei Chang, and Polle Zellweger. Fluid visualization for spreadsheet structures. In *Visual Languages*, pages 118–125, 1998.

[52] D. Ingalls, S. Wallace, Y.-Y. Chow, F. Ludolph, and K. Doyle. Fabrick: A visual programming environment. In *Proc. OOPSLA '88*, pages 176–190, September 1988.

[53] Alfred Inselberg. Multidimensional detective. In *Proceedings of the Symposium on Information Visualization '97*, pages 100–107. IEEE CS, 1997. Phoenix, Arizona.

[54] IRIS Explorer home page. http://www.nag.co.uk/Welcome_IEC.html, February 1999.

[55] T. J. Jankun-Kelly and Kwan-Liu Ma. Visualization exploration and encapsulation via a spreadsheet-like interface. *IEEE Transactions on Visualization and Computer Graphics*, 7(3):275–287, 2001.

[56] Brian Johnson and Ben Shneiderman. Tree-maps: A space-filling approach to the visualization of hierarchical information structures. In *Proc. IEEE Visualization '91*, pages 284–291. IEEE CS, 1991.

[57] Colleen M. Kehoe and James E. Pitkow. Emerging trends in the www user population. *Communications of the ACM*, 39(6), 1996.

[58] Frank Kriwaczek. LogiCalc—a Prolog spreadsheet. In Bob Kowalski and Frank Kriwaczek, editors, *Logic Programming*, pages 105–117. Addison-Wesley, 1986.

[59] John Lamping, Ramana Rao, and Peter Pirolli. A focus+context technique based on hyperbolic geometry for visualizing large hierarchies. In *Proceedings of ACM CHI'95 Conference on Human Factors in Computing Systems*, volume 1, pages 401–408, 1995.

[60] John Peter Lee and Georges G. Grinstein. An architecture for retaining and analyzing visual explorations of databases. In *Proc. IEEE Visualization '95*, pages 101–108. IEEE CS, 1995. Atlanta, Georgia.

[61] K. Lee. *Interactive Computer Graphics in Architecture*. Environmental Design & Research Center, Boston, 1976.

[62] Y. K. Leung and M. D. Apperley. A review and taxonomy of distortion-oriented presentation techniques. *ACM Transactions on Computer-Human Interaction*, 1(2):126–160, 1994.

[63] Marc Levoy. Spreadsheets for images. In Andrew Glassner, editor, *Proceedings of SIGGRAPH '94 (Orlando, Florida, July 24–29, 1994)*, Computer Graphics Proceedings, Annual Conference Series, pages 139–146. ACM SIGGRAPH, ACM Press, July 1994. ISBN 0-89791-667-0.

[64] T. V. Loudon, J. F. Wheeler, and K. P. Andrew. Affine transformations for digitized spatial data in geology. *Comput. Geosci.*, pages 397–412, 1980.

[65] Jock Mackinlay. Automating the design of graphical presentation of relational information. *ACM Transaction on Graphics*, 5(2):110–141, April 1986.

[66] Jock D. Mackinlay, George G. Robertson, and Stuart K. Card. The Perspective Wall: Detail and context smoothly integrated. In *Proceedings of ACM CHI'91 Conference on Human Factors in Computing Systems*, pages 173–179, 1991.

[67] B. McCormick et al. Visualization in scientific computing. In *Computer Graphics*, volume 21. ACM Press, November 1987.

[68] Sougata Mukherjea, James D. Foley, and Scott Hudson. Visualizing complex hypermedia networks through multiple hierarchical views. In *Proceedings of ACM CHI'95 Conference on Human Factors in Computing Systems*, volume 1, pages 331–337, 1995.

[69] Brad A. Myers. Graphical techniques in a spreadsheet for specifying user interfaces. In *Proceedings of ACM CHI'91 Conference on Human Factors in Computing Systems*, pages 243–249, 1991.

[70] Brad A. Myers, Dario A. Giuse, Roger B. Dannenberg, Brad Vander Zanden, David S. Kosbie, Ed Pervin, Andrew Mickish, and Philippe Marchal. Comprehensive support for graphical, highly-interactive user interfaces: The Garnet user interface development environment. *IEEE Computer*, 23(11):71–85, November 1990.

[71] David Nation, C. Plaisant, G. Marchioinini, and A. Komlodi. Visualizing websites using a hierarchical table of contents browser: WebTOC. In *Proceedings of 3rd Conference on Human Factors and the Web*, 1997. http://www.uswest.com/web-conference/proceedings/nation.html.

[72] National Center for Biotechnology Information. http://www.ncbi.nlm.nih.gov/.

[73] Greg Nelson. Juno, A constraint-based graphics system. In B. A. Barsky, editor, *Computer Graphics (SIGGRAPH '85 Proceedings)*, volume 19, pages 235–243, July 1985.

[74] Donald A. Norman. *The Design of Everyday Things*. Doubleday, 1988.

[75] M. V. Olson. The human genome project. *Proc Natl Acad Sci U S A*, 90(10):4338–4344, 1993.

[76] John K. Ousterhout. *Tcl and the Tk Toolkit*. Addison-Wesley, 1994.

[77] K. W. Piersol. Object-oriented spreadsheets: The Analytic Spreadsheet Package. In Norman Meyrowitz, editor, *Proceedings of the Conference on Object-Oriented Programming Systems, Languages, and Applications (OOPSLA)*, pages 385–390, Portland, OR USA, November 1986. ACM Press. Published as SIGPLAN Notices, volume 21, number 11.

[78] Peter Pirolli and Stuart Card. Information foraging in information access environments. In *Proceedings of ACM CHI'95 Conference on Human Factors in Computing Systems*, volume 1, pages 51–58, 1995.

[79] Peter Pirolli, James Pitkow, and Ramana Rao. Silk from a sow's ear: Extracting usable structure from the web. In *Proceedings of ACM CHI 96 Conference on Human Factors in Computing Systems*, volume 1, pages 118–125, 1996.

[80] James E. Pitkow and Krishna Bharat. WebViz: A tool for world wide web access log visualization. In *Proceedings of the First International World Wide Web Conference*, May 1994. Geneva, Switzerland.

[81] T. K. Porter. The shaded surface display of large molecules. In *Computer Graphics (SIGGRAPH '79 Proceedings)*, volume 13, pages 234–236, August 1979.

[82] David Potter. *Computational Physics*. John Wiley and Sons, 1973.

[83] Ramana Rao and Stuart K. Card. The Table Lens: Merging graphical and symbolic representations in an interactive focus+context visualization for tabular information. In *Proceedings of ACM CHI'94 Conference on Human Factors in Computing Systems*, volume 1, pages 318–322, 1994. Color plates on pages 481-482.

[84] Ramana Rao and Stuart K. Card. Exploring large tables with the Table Lens. In *Proceedings of ACM CHI'95 Conference on Human Factors in Computing Systems*, volume 2, pages 403–404, 1995.

[85] Craig W. Reynolds. Flocks, herds, and schools: A distributed behavioral model. In Maureen C. Stone, editor, *Computer Graphics (SIGGRAPH '87 Proceedings)*, volume 21, pages 25–34, July 1987.

[86] George G. Robertson and Jock D. Mackinlay. The Document Lens. In *Proceedings of the ACM SIGGRAPH Symposium on User Interface Software and Technology*, pages 101–108, 1993.

[87] George G. Robertson, Jock D. Mackinlay, and Stuart K. Card. Cone Trees: Animated 3D visualizations of hierarchical information. In *Proceedings of ACM CHI'91 Conference on Human Factors in Computing Systems*, pages 189–194, 1991.

[88] Daniel M. Russell, Mark J. Stefik, Peter Pirolli, and Stuart K. Card. The cost structure of sensemaking. In *Proceedings of ACM INTERCHI'93 Conference on Human Factors in Computing Systems*, pages 269–276, 1993.

[89] Manojit Sarkar and Marc H. Brown. Graphical fisheye views of graphs. In *Proceedings of ACM CHI'92 Conference on Human Factors in Computing Systems*, pages 83–91, 1992.

[90] Manojit Sarkar, Scott S. Snibbe, Oren J. Tversky, and Steven P. Reiss. Stretching the rubber sheet: A metophor for visualizing large layouts on small screens. In *Proceedings of the ACM SIGGRAPH Symposium on User Interface Software and Technology*, pages 81–91, 1993.

[91] William J. Schroeder, Kenneth M. Martin, and William E. Lorensen. The design and implementation of an object-oriented toolkit for 3D graphics and visualization. In Roni Yagel and Gregory M. Nielson, editors, *Proc. IEEE Visualization '96*, pages 93–100. IEEE CS Press, 1996. San Francisco, California.

[92] William J. Schroeder, Kenneth M. Martin, and William E. Lorensen. *The Visualization Toolkit: An Object-Oriented Approach to 3D Graphics*. Prentice Hall, 1996.

[93] Herbert A. Simon. *The Sciences of the Artificial*. MIT Press, 1969.

[94] Michael Spenke and Christian Beilken. A spreadsheet interface for logic programming. In *Proceedings of ACM CHI'89 Conference on Human Factors in Computing Systems*, pages 75–80, 1989.

[95] Michael Spenke, Christian Beilken, and Thomas Berlage. FOCUS: The interactive table for product comparison and selection. In *Proceedings of the ACM Symposium on User Interface Software and Technology*, pages 41–50, 1996.

[96] Marc Stadelmann. A spreadsheet based on constraints. In *Proceedings of the ACM SIGGRAPH Symposium on User Interface Software and Technology*, pages 217–224, 1993.

[97] Maureen C. Stone, Ken Fishkin, and Eric A. Bier. The movable filter as a user interface tool. In *Proceedings of ACM CHI'94 Conference on Human Factors in Computing Systems*, volume 1, pages 306–312, 1994.

[98] Silicon Graphics Computer Systems. *IRIS Explorer User's Guide*. Silicon Graphics Computer Systems, Mountain View, CA, 1991.

[99] Tom Newman et al. A Summary of Methods for Accessing Results from Large-Scale Partial Sequencing of Anonymous *Arabidopsis* cDNA Clones. *Plant Physiology*, 106:1241–1255, 1994.

[100] Lloyd A. Treinish. Visualization of stratospheric ozone depletion and the polar vortex. Technical report, IBM Thomas J. Watson Research Center, 1996.

[101] Edward Tufte. *The Visual Display of Quantitative Information*. Graphics Press, Cheshire, Connecticut, 1992.

[102] Lisa Tweedie. Characterizing interactive externalizations. In *Proceedings of ACM CHI 97 Conference on Human Factors in Computing Systems*, volume 1, pages 375–382, 1997.

[103] Craig Upson, Jr. Thomas Faulhaber, David Kamins, David Laidlaw, David Schlegel, Jeffery Vroom, Robert Gurwitz, and Andries van Dam. The Application Visualization System: A computational environment for scientific visualization. *IEEE Computer Graphics and Applications*, pages 30–42, July 1989.

[104] M. H. van Emden, M. Ohki, and A. Takeuchi. Spreadsheets with incremental queries as a user interface for logic programming. Technical Report TR-144, ICOT, 1985.

[105] J.J. van Wijke and R. van Liere. Hyperslice: Visualization of scalar functions of many variable. In *Proc. IEEE Visualization '91*, pages 119–125, Los Altimos, CA, 1991. IEEE CS.

[106] Amitabh Varshney and Arie Kaufman. FINESSE: A financial information spreadsheet. In *Proceedings of the Symposium on Information Visualization '96*, pages 70–71, 125. IEEE CS, 1996. San Francisco, California.

[107] Visible Decisions. Visible Decisions, Inc. http://www.vdi.com, January 1999.

[108] E. M. Wilcox, J. W. Atwood, M. M. Burnett, J. J. Cadiz, and C. R. Cook. Does continuous visual feedback aid debugging in direct-manipulation programming systems? In *ACM Proceedings CHI'97: Human Factors in Computing Systems*, pages 258–265, March 1997.

[109] Nicholas Wilde and Clayton Lewis. Spreadsheet-based interactive graphics: From prototype to tool. In *Proceedings of ACM CHI'90 Conference on Human Factors in Computing Systems*, pages 153–159, 1990.

[110] Graham Wills and John Dill, editors. *Proceedings of the Symposium on Information Visualization '98*. IEEE CS, 1998. Research Triangle Park, North Carolina.

[111] James A. Wise, James J. Thomas, Kelly Pennock, David Lantrip, Marc Pottier, Anne Schur, and Vern Crow. Visualizing the non-visual: Spatial analysis and interaction with information from text documents. In *Proceedings of the Symposium on Information Visualization '95*, pages 51–58. IEEE CS, 1995. Atlanta, Georgia.

[112] Brad Vander Zanden, Brad A. Myers, Dario Giuse, and Pedro Szekely. The importance of pointer variables in constraint models. In *Proceedings of the ACM SIGGRAPH Symposium on User Interface Software and Technology*, pages 155–164, 1991.

Index

MIX
Papier aus verantwortungsvollen Quellen
Paper from responsible sources
FSC® C105338

If you have any concerns about our products,
you can contact us on
ProductSafety@springernature.com

In case Publisher is established outside the EU,
the EU authorized representative is:
Springer Nature Customer Service Center GmbH
Europaplatz 3, 69115 Heidelberg, Germany

Printed by Libri Plureos GmbH
in Hamburg, Germany